CONTENTS

Contributors
The posts and positions held by contributors at the time of the delivery of the
paper are given here, though since then some have taken office elsewhere.
Professor Hargreaves is now in Cambridge University, Professor Aspin in
Monash University, Australia. Sadly, John Blacking died recently after a period
of illness.

THE ARTS AND EDUCATION

PAPERS FROM
THE NATIONAL ASSOCIATION FOR EDUCATION IN THE ARTS
1983 - 1990

:DITED BY PROFESSOR KEITH SWANWICK

'ITUTE OF EDUCATION, UNIVERSITY OF LONDON

Published by the National Association for Education in the Arts

© *NAEA 1990*

ISBN 0-9511714-2-9

British Library Cataloguing in Publication Data
The Arts and Education: papers from the National Association for Education
in the Arts 1983-1990
1. Great Britain. Educational Institutions. Curriculum subjects. Arts
I. Swanwick, Keith II. National Association for Education in the Arts
700.71041

ISBN 0-9511714-2-9

Printed by Unwin Brothers Limited
The Gresham Press, Old Woking, Surrey GU22 9LH
A MEMBER OF THE MARTINS PRINTING GROUP

EDITORIAL INTRODUCTION

The National Association for Education in the Arts was founded in 1983 to promote and advance the understanding, practice and status of the arts in education - dance, drama, music, the visual arts, literature and media. Since then, NAEA has been an influential forum, facilitating exchange of views across the arts and has contributed to decision-making at all levels.

The series of conferences organised between 1983 and 1990 gave rise to a number of publications; sometimes single papers, sometimes a set of papers, sometimes reports of conference discussions. In this book, THE ARTS AND EDUCATION, we have collected together some of the most significant of these papers, reordering them to into three main sections which address major issues, The Arts and the School Curriculum, Assessment and the Arts, The Arts Beyond the Curriculum.

The contributors include politicians, teachers in schools and people in Higher Education. Between them they represent a wide diversity of experience and several differing perspectives on the arts and education. What they share is commitment to the arts and a belief that education has a crucial part to play in facilitating access to the arts.

The concerns, ideas and arguments here presented will surely extend beyond the decade of the '80's.

Keith Swanwick

Institute of Education, University of London

Chair of NAEA, 1987-1990

PART ONE

THE ARTS AND THE CURRICULUM

These papers, including a substantial address by the Minister of State for Education, Angela Rumbold, deal with issues of fundamental as well as topical importance. They originated at a lively conference in October, 1987, which helped to clarify where arts educators need to be looking for future development in relationship to the National Curriculum. In addition to the addresses from the platform by the Minister and by Derek Fatchett for the Labour Party, by myself and David Hargreaves, there were vigorous questions and comments from the floor which elicited from Angela Rumbold reaffirmation of points made during her presentation.

ANGELA RUMBOLD, MINISTER OF STATE FOR EDUCATION

I was very happy to be asked by Kenneth Baker (then Secretary of State for Education) to represent him at your annual conference. As you know, the Government is about to introduce a Bill in Parliament which proposes a number of important changes to education. Today I want to concentrate on our proposals for a National Curriculum.

I know that this audience will be particularly interested in the implications for 'The Arts', so I will focus attention on this aspect of the curriculum. Your Association understands by 'The Arts', dance, drama, music, the visual arts, literature and media. It seems to me sensible to follow these broad categories also when I explain to you our proposals, and how these parts of the curriculum will be affected by what we are trying to do. I also want to make clear my own personal commitment to education in the arts.

I hope that most of you will have seen a copy of our Consultation Document on the National Curriculum. Like many best sellers it is not short-listed for the Booker Prize. But perhaps that is also because it isn't fiction! We have sent out over 60, 000 copies and I have arranged for a number of copies to be available before lunch. I have also arranged to have copies here of the important letters to the Maths and Science Subject Working Groups, and the press release about the setting up of the Task Group on Assessment and Testing (TGAT). I know that these documents help clarify a number of important points about which there have been some misconceptions.

The first point to which I wish to draw your attention is that our proposals envisage that *all pupils* throughout their time in compulsory schooling should have a broad and balanced curriculum. It is particularly important that these involved in education in the arts should understand this clearly.

Of course the idea that a properly balanced curriculum should have adequate provision for the arts has a long history. The ancient Greeks insisted that music, as well as literature and music, continued to be an important part of the *Trivium* and *Quadrivium*, the two stages in which the curriculum was divided in the West from Roman times through the middle Ages to the Renaissance. Quite recently, in our own country, we have had the benefit of a well-argued reminder of the need for balanced curricular provision for the arts in the Gulbenkian Foundation's Report on *The Arts in Schools* (1982).

In welcoming this Report, Keith Joseph, who was then secretary of State for Education and Science, described it as making a cogent case for the arts in the school curriculum. And later, in the subsequent debate on the Report in the House of Lords, Lord Elton, speaking for the Government, described the arts not merely as 'desirable', but as *'an essential component of the education offered in schools'*.

There is no doubt that this Report led to a better understanding of the issues, and to more co-ordinated effort. An important catalyst has been the School

Curriculum Development Committee's Project 'The Arts in Schools'. I am glad to be able to pay tribute here to the valuable work it has done. This project has been carried out in partnership with a large number of LEAs, and gives practical support to teacher, schools, and the authorities themselves, in developing provision for the arts. We have made it clear that we expect this valuable project to continue under the auspices of the new National Curriculum Council.

Of course it is true that a core curriculum of Maths, English and Science puts a heavy emphasis on the scientific and numerate side of education. Some could argue that the inclusion of technology as a foundation subject will serve to increase this emphasis to the point where our objective of balance could be at risk.

I think such a view would be wrong, and I want to explain why. There are good reasons for the emphasis on numeracy and science in the core curriculum. We need to be sure that all pupils, from their earliest time at school, have a good grounding in mathematical skills. Even if their subsequent career is to be in some aspect of the arts, it is important that they have solid grounding, both to cope with everyday life, and to help them in their work. I suspect that there may be some people in the arts world who would manage the business side of their careers better if they felt more at ease with figures. I am sure too that many of you can think of aspects of your work, or the future work of your pupils, where maths will be vital. That is why we are so keen that pupils continue to study right through their period of compulsory schooling. Allowing pupils to drop subjects which are important for their future careers because they find them difficult is not doing them a service. And, in any case, of course, there are many mathematicians who would put mathematics on the arts' side of the curriculum.

Science has a similar importance. It is essential because scientific developments seems likely to continue to have a major impact on our world. It is vital therefore that all our young people should be at ease with its concepts. But science and technology are exerting and increasing influence on the world of the arts as well. Here I am thinking of the range of new materials available for work in the visual arts, of developments in electronic music, as well as of the general impact of computers across all subjects.

But the point I want to stress is that alongside this requirement for our pupils to be numerate, and to know about scientific principles, there is a vital requirement to develop the aesthetic and design sense. A very good example of how the aesthetic and scientific come together is design, not least when it is coupled with technology of which it is an essential feature. It is important that *more* of our manufacturers turn out products which are both well fitted for their purpose *and* have aesthetic appeal so that they compete effectively in the market place with products from other countries.

Education has an important part to play in developing the necessary awareness of good design, and the skills needed to achieve this. Good design is especially important for technology, but it needs to inform the whole curriculum. It is one of the essential cross-curricular themes. A good understanding of design is important for everyone: for scientists, for those engaged in commerce or in the professions, or in other walks of life. And a sense of what is good design is invaluable for many aspects of life where aesthetic discrimination is important.

Of course, the need to develop the aesthetic values and skills of pupils goes much wider than just making sure that we improve our design capability. But what I have tried to illustrate is that the polarisation of maths, science and technology versus the rest is false, and that our aim of making sure that these subjects get proper attention at all phases of education does not imply less regard for the arts. When the issues are considered more closely, I suggest that we may see the relevance and contribution of sciences generally to arts education.

And I have not yet mentioned English, which is one of the core subjects of the national curriculum, and is one of the finest jewels in 'The Arts' crown. Here I want to make it quite clear that there is no intention of diminishing English to the point where it is a mere means of oral communication. When the English Working Group is appointed at around the turn of the year, it is our intention to ensure that the advice it receives on drawing up attainment targets and programmes of study will encourage a *broad approach* to the teaching of English. We will ensure that drama and English literature, including poetry, are given their proper place.

Of course, it is vital that our pupils can communicate effectively when they speak and when they write. Many of them may increasingly do the latter at the keyboard rather than with a pen, although I would still favour efforts being made to encourage pupils to improve their *handwriting*. Yet I believe we should at the same time welcome the way in which various kinds of word processor can help children to gain confidence in the use of words, and not just for utilitarian purposes. And it is essential that they should also become acquainted with the great tradition of our literature of all periods, including our own, and that they learn to write imaginatively and creatively themselves as well. They should learn to narrate, describe, analyse, persuade and inform, in a variety of styles to meet the needs of their reader.

I also want to say a little more about drama. Some of you may regret that it is not a foundation subject on its own. But I would like to make clear here the importance we attach to it, both in its own right, and for the contribution it can make to other parts of the curriculum. For in many ways drama can be seen as an area of experience which can help pupils *right across the foundation subjects.* The techniques of speaking effectively on stage, or even learning to read a part in class, can be of enormous benefit to pupils in presenting themselves, and in developing the confidence to put across their ideas effectively, both in class, outside school, and later in adult life. The experience of feeling your way into a part, of sensing the emotions and conflicts of another person, can help develop the personal skills and empathy which we want children to acquire. This can also help them in their understanding of both people and events in history and literature. Some experience of drama can be just as useful to salesman, teachers (whatever their subject specialisms), and businessmen, as well as to politicians. Many of our technocrats and bureaucrats could probably do with having had more of it.

I am therefore particularly glad that drama in schools is an area where a lot of work has been and is being done by local authorities. The way in which drama has been used to help children gain a more vivid understanding of history when they visit the Wigan Pier Heritage Museum, is particularly interesting. Projects to take actors into schools to enliven teaching, school visits to the theatre - I would want to encourage *all* such efforts to use drama to enrich the curriculum of children in our schools. Another example is the work being done by the museum service at Quarry Bank Mill at Styal in Cheshire. This is also seeking to help children's education through involving them in active work in drama.

May I now turn to two of the subjects which have been included as foundation subjects: Music and Art. I believe the way in which music has developed in our schools has been one of the most exciting features of education in recent years. The range of musical experience in our primary and secondary schools, the amazingly high standards of many of our young performers, the quantity and quality of music making which is going on in such a high proportion of schools is truly remarkable. It is a great credit to the dedication of music teachers, many of whom not only inspire their pupils, but also other members of staff to get involved in music in their schools.

We want to see this enthusiasm for music continue to flower, once music becomes a foundation subject. As you know, we have not suggested that there should be attainment targets for music. But we do propose to issue guidelines, and there will be programmes of study. We will be looking to advice on what they should contain from the working group of those involved in musical education. No doubt some of them may be members of this Association although membership of the Subject Working Groups will not be on a representative basis. Our aim will be to bring all pupils throughout their primary and secondary school years, into contact with the musicians' fundamental activities in a wide range of different kinds of music - performing, singing or playing an instrument, or listening. I would also hope they would gain some experience in musical composition itself.

We in central government will continue to do what we can to help give music in schools the encouragement it deserves. As many of you will know, the Department, on Kenneth Baker's initiative, supported a National Choral Competition in July this year, organised by 'Music for Youth' as part of their annual national festival, to serve as a shop window to display the excellence of *choral work* being achieved by pupils in maintained schools. This competition proved to be a great success, and we are going to support it again next year. The Schools Prom, which I attended with great pleasure last year and which is to be held on 23-25 November this year at the Royal Albert Hall, is another example of the rich range of music making we are keen to encourage. This will involve young musicians from all parts of the country in all types of instrumental and vocal ensembles.

The National Association for Primary Education are to be congratulated too on the Festival of Children's Voices they held this year. There are many other national and local occasions which demonstrate how schools have built up a tradition of which they can be justly proud.

I have already mentioned the importance we attach to an understanding of design in the curriculum as a whole. It will of course, continue to have important links with Art. This brings me to my own particular interest. Work in the visual arts has always been one of the strengths of our primary and secondary schools. And this is a good opportunity to pay tribute to the work of a number of local education authorities, who have funded the establishment of loan and handling collections, as part of their general support for the visual arts in their areas. I would also like to commend the work of National bodies like the Crafts, Arts and Design Councils, the regional arts associations, museums and galleries, which have been involved in numerous initiatives to help enrich children's education in the visual arts. And I am delighted industry is also increasingly seeing the importance of supporting visual arts education. A good example of this is Cadbury's sponsorship of the National Exhibition of Children's Art, which Kenneth Baker is opening on 18 November.

Art is also to be one of the foundation subjects. It will have programmes of study, and guidelines or attainment objectives. We will be looking to those involved in education in the arts to advise the Working Group when it is set up, on what should be in these for the different stages of a child's career in school.

My survey of the arts in schools would be incomplete without a reference to dance. We see this as an important part of the physical education of our pupils. Although this has been a part of the physical education in primary schools, it is its progress in secondary schools in the last fifteen years which has been particularly remarkable. Of course, there is also a case for seeing dance as part of the creative, expressive and performing arts. This is another area where it should be rewarding to establish links between the different areas of the curriculum so that each can benefit from the other. We shall certainly bear this in mind when issuing guidance for the Working Groups.

But will there be *time* to cover all those aspects of the arts we should all like to see in the school curriculum? This point has been frequently brought to my attention as I have been travelling about the country in the last few months. After all, the Consultation Document gives some illustrations as to the percentage of time which is being allocated to the foundation subjects in the last years of compulsory schooling. That reflects much good practice.

But the first point I would make is that we do not propose to lay down the amount of time for the foundation subjects in statute. The second is the amount of time which will be available for non-foundation subjects will be about 20 per cent. Moreover, teachers themselves will have considerable flexibility to draw up schemes of work both for the foundation subjects and other areas of learning and skills. We are not in the business of telling schools how to operate and deliver the curriculum, or dictating the school timetable. All we are saying is that however the curriculum is organised it must contain the programmes of study, and prepare pupils for the attainment targets where these are specified.

Teachers should think imaginatively about schemes of work for their schools. They will need to do this to ensure that what is essential in their subjects is covered. Inevitably choices must be made. That is an essential result of the decision we have confirmed, after a 10 year debate, that every child is entitled to a broad and balanced curriculum. So all teachers in the arts, as well as in other disciplines will have to take a view of what it is that is *essential* that pupils should *know*, *understand* and be able to *do*. For many of the arts subjects, teachers will need to decide what are the vital aesthetic experiences to which all pupils need to be exposed.

I do not pretend that this is easy. But I have every confidence that arts teachers will respond to this challenge.

I have now been through a number of arts subjects individually. I want at this point to suggest that there is also an advantage in considering 'the arts' as a whole, as your Association does. For a number of the arts subjects can benefit from being grouped together. Sometimes we see this happening creatively, so that a new art form emerges, I am thinking here of opera, in which music, drama and the visual arts, and sometimes dance - and very frequently design and technology - all come together. And this has happened without damaging the integrity of the underlying art forms, which still flourish separately.

I believe that the same thing can also happen in education in the arts. It is for consideration whether there may not be benefit in courses where the individual arts subjects are studied alongside each other. Each one is capable of providing insight into the others. This is one of the possibilities which is envisaged for years 4 and 5 in the Consultation Document. This approach would link in well with the useful work which is going on in TVEI for the 14-19 year olds on inter-related arts courses.

TVEI has also been one of the ways in which the so-called twentieth century art forms, film, radio and television for media studies have been developed in the curriculum. Following the introduction of '*Popular TV and School Children*', a report by a group of teachers, a number of regional working groups have been established to promote this particular area of arts work. The Department is now supporting this with a grant administered by the British Film Institute.

All in all, such developments will also link in well with the courses being offered at polytechnics and colleges of higher education which lead to qualifications in the performing and expressive arts.

Looked at as a whole, then I believe that our proposals for a National Curriculum will serve to underpin much of the important work which is going on in education in the arts, both during primary and secondary school, and beyond.

I want now to share with you some thoughts about the contribution which the arts in general can make to the development of a child as a rounded person. There has been some attempt to portray the National Curriculum as something rather soulless.

The emphasis that has been placed on maths and science, and the fact that the Working Groups in these subjects have been established first, may have contributed to this. The first point I would make is that we have made it very clear in the letter to the Chairmen of the first two Subject Working Groups, that we expect them to take account of the need for all elements of the curriculum to contribute to the development of general personal and social qualities.

We have also made very clear the importance we attach to Religious Education, which is at present the only subject which is required to be taught by law. And I would add here that the contribution which the arts can make to enhancing pupils' spiritual development has always been enormous, and will continue to be so. We are also quite clear that much work in the arts demands intellectual understanding of a very high order. Anyone who has tried to write a book, or score a piece of music, knows that well. Education in the arts also helps develop the creative sense - the kind of lateral and imaginative thinking which is so important in solving the complex problems of modern life. And because many aspects of them demand practical, physical skills of a very high order, it represents a useful training for many aspects of life where these skills are of value. But in addition it encourages that kind of self discipline and persistence in the pursuit of difficulties which are an important part of the development of character.

There is one further aspect of education in the arts which I want to focus on particularly. This is the contribution which it can make to children's emotional development. A National Curriculum, which *simply* turned out children who had first rate numeracy and scientific skills, would not be one which any of us would want. And pupils, teachers and parent would rightly rebel against if it ever came into being. In my view it is education in the arts which makes a significant contribution to the way children develop their feelings and understand their emotions. It is this part of the curriculum which can play the most significant part in ensuring that children, when they leave school, and go out into adult life and employment, have developed emotionally in a way which complements the intellectual knowledge and skills which we all hope they will acquire. The arts then will also have provided a precious foundation which can be developed throughout their lives as adults, and can be a continuing source of inspiration, pleasure and excitement.

In conclusion I hope I have drawn together for you the essential elements of how we see the individual parts of the Arts being presented to school children whilst at the same time ensuring that they cover all important aspects of the separate elements. We must not overload the curriculum but we must ensure that the Arts fit well into our concept of a broad and balanced one.

But let there be no misunderstanding of our objectives. Education in the Arts is a fundamental part of our educational proposals for the curriculum. Without it we would be allowing our children to have missed a huge area of enrichment during their years in school, and an essential preparation for all that lies before them in their adult life.

DEREK FATCHETT, LABOUR PARTY SPOKESMAN ON EDUCATION

I would like to begin by focusing my attention on the philosophy behind the National Curriculum and make comments in that direction.

It was the Government's own Arts Minister Mr Richard Luce who said that Drama, Literature, Music, Arts and Craft all played an important role both in personal education and within the developing curriculum. That is a view we would simply share and it is a view that would underpin my approach to the curriculum and educational philosophy. I totally reject the notion that education can be seen as a massive process and contribution towards National Manpower Planning. I think that is wrong. I think that it is wrong philosophy in the sense that it sees teaching in very limited and very restrictive ways. I think it is also naive in terms of manpower planning, because what we are told by the experts is that what we need in terms of skills for the economy in 1987 we will not necessarily need in 1997 and the year 2007. What we will need in 20 years time will be people who are flexible, able to adapt and I would have thought that the National Curriculum would aim to achieve these objectives and also to provide in the process somewhat better manpower planning. So we will be guided to a certain extent by educational practice and what we have achieved and I have listened with some interest to the discussion about dance.

I come from Leeds and have within my Labour Party constituency, teachers from Harehills Middle School in Leeds. I have certain views from experience and I find that a very refreshing one is the importance of dance in terms of the life of the school, because what happened at Harehills Middle School is that teachers with vision, with commitment and with the ability to change the mind of the Headteacher were able to introduce dance as a compulsory part of the middle school curriculum so that children had dance as part of their work at school. Now Yorkshire folk are funny folk in this respect and there were those who said, 'It won't work', and 'It is not what we want our lads to be doing'. But, of course, it worked and it worked because it broke down stereotypes. It broke down stereotypes on a gender basis. The boys turned out to enjoy it much more that the girls and the boys turned out to be the professional dancers because out of one small acorn grew Phoenix Dance, Northern Contemporary Dance and of course, it also broke down racial stereotypes in that Asian youngsters. Afro-Caribbean youngsters and white youngsters joined in and worked together. Now that can happen in a school because there was flexibility. There was the opportunity to be flexible and I think that is important when we approach the educational process and approach out thinking about the National Curriculum. What worries me about the Government's proposal, (and I welcomed a lot of what the Minister said previously in terms of flexibility and consultation and I hope that proves to be the case in practice) but what worries me about it is that it is very hard in terms of its current definition of what is the central core and what is the flexible part of the National Curriculum. You see we have got a

90:10 distribution. I suspect if all of us sent down to the greengrocers and bought an apple with 90% core and 10% fruit we would take it back. I see the National Curriculum somewhat in these terms because the 10% fruit is where educational advancement and development take place, so I worry about it being restrictive in that sense.

I worry about it being restrictive in another sense in that *process* seems to have been forgotten and subjects seem to have come back on the agenda. Now I am of the age, Chairman, sad to say, that I can look back and see in this my own school timetable. It was that dreadful first Monday morning of term when the timetable came and you had the blocks and in these blocks you thought about Science or Latin or whatever it was and your mind was not allowed to drift in any other direction. Now I think teachers in education have advanced very substantially from that, towards a *process* which enables youngsters to bring together subjects and to interact around subjects and around topics. That is very important, and the National Curriculum document to me does not address that advance. I always quote a letter from a teacher which was in *The Independent* in August. It was a wonderful letter because it was written by a teacher within my constituency, (but not stimulated by me), but if it came from Leeds then, therefore, it must have some basic merit. But she wrote a letter very crucial to the argument in which she said that she had a group of 9 year olds who had written an essay on Jesus. They then put that onto a word processor and had it printed out and they'd drawn together skills, and she wanted to know whether that was RE, IT, or English. I'm very worried that if we have slabs of subjects only, excellent process in teaching practice will be lost to us and, therefore, I would approach the National Curriculum with that scepticism.

I would also worry about it in relation to testing, because it does seem to me and I have listened once or twice to the minister and read what she has to say with great interest. (I also listened the other night in the House of Commons to what one or two Conservative back benchers had to say.) I do not think that the Government has determined clearly whether we are talking about diagnostic testing or competitive testing and we need to know the answer to that. If it is diagnostic testing then of course nobody disagrees because all good schools diagnostically test children regularly. I take the Minister's point that information should be given on those tests to parents but then I would have thought that good educational practice would encourage that, and that it should be part of good educational practice, but there is a world of difference between diagnostic testing and competitive testing and I worry greatly about the education system that is going to create benchmarks of failure at the ages of 7, 11 and 14.

My very simple view is that if you get to the age of 7 and fail you will be deemed a failure for the next nine years and that is a massive waste of talent and resources. So I hope that we can persuade the Government even if we cannot persuade the Prime Minister, that there is good educational argument for diagnostic testing but no educational argument at all for competitive testing. But, of course, if we have competitive testing it is the primary schools and the arts which will be most badly affected by that change. Children will be affected, so will teaching, because what will happen in the process is that teachers will be pushed by parental pressure to teach towards a pass in those examinations, rather than towards a broad enhancement of individual ability and individual talent and I feel that that is going to restrict what goes on in the primary schools to a very great extent, and indeed restrict what happens in the secondary schools. If we are going to develop the whole person, which I see as part of education, then we need to develop that whole person not in an atmosphere in which testing a class is going to be the key characteristic. If we look at some of the comments that have come from the Hillgate Group which some may dismiss - (I am not sure whether the Minister would dismiss) - the Hillgate Group on the far right of the Conservative Party write tomorrow's agenda for education and the way things are going at the moment they write the Prime Minister's agenda for today. The Hillgate Group want competitive testing, they want schools to be compared, they want Local Authorities to be compared. That is naive but dangerous and certainly dangerous for our children and what goes on in the classroom. So we reject all forms of competitive testing.

If I can, Chairman, I would like to go on to another area which worries me about the National Curriculum. There is no identification process. There is no identification, it seems to me, in the way the document is written, of children who do not fall in the top 15 to 20%. I have read this document a number of times. I have talked to many teachers up and down the country, many parents' groups and it does seem to me that the whole document is couched in a language where all children are going to fall into that to 15 or 20% and be taught in a particular way. It is a gift that this Government has. It is a peculiar characteristic of the Prime Minister. It is statistically incorrect, of course, because I have never worked out how all children can fall into the top 15 - 20% (maybe my lack of numeracy will be partly the reason for that), but I think there are other reasons. But is worrying in other respects because what the Government seems to be implying time after time is that if your child doesn't come into that top 15 - 20%, it is not the Government's fault, they have only been in for 8 years. They are not at all responsible for running the education system, nothing at all to do with them - anything wrong is not at all their responsibility, it is not the Government's fault. It may be the fault of your LEA and it certainly may be the fault of teachers.

I think we need a much more adult and mature philosophy that talks about the needs of all our children, not just those that come within the top 15 - 20%. Again if you look at developments that have taken place in education, one of them is recognising that we don't all come within the top 15 - 20%. It is recognising that you have to maintain interest amongst youngsters. You have to give youngsters the opportunity to achieve and to attain. Not all of our youngsters will achieve and attain within the same subject areas, the same topics. There will be a breadth in terms of our talents. That is a good thing. There will be breadth in terms of our attainment and I would hope that we can push the educational debate forward not just to talk about 'the top of this or that', but to make statements about the special needs of those other youngsters in whom we have to maintain interest until the age of 16. And what has happened in craft design and technology in the arts has maintained interest for a lot of youngsters until the age of 16, because they have been able to create in a world in which many of them feel it is difficult to create.

One of the things that I think those of us who comment on education have to recognise is that, as in the world outside, there are immense cynical pressures upon our youngsters which the schools have done a good job to combat. I meet youngsters whom I talk to when I go around schools in my own constituency at the ages of 13 or 14. All of them will say to me, when I try to encourage them in ways which may be paternal and outdated, 'Well, what is there to do? My older brother Johnny, or sister Jane are on YTS. Don't need to do much to get on YTS', they will say. We have got to maintain their interest until the age of 16 and I sometimes wonder whether this particular National Curriculum document ever recognises that there is that problem in maintaining interest.

So we approach the National Curriculum with that educational philosophy of developing a focus of education (and I use the word very carefully) as a process that persuades people to ask the subversive question. I am one of those - and I hope that the Daily Mail or Daily Express isn't here - and I use that word in a very strict sense because education should persuade us not to just find out how things happen, but why things happen. The whole educational process should be directed towards getting our youngster to ask 'Why?' subversive question in that sense, 'Why this thing happens in our society', 'Why this happens in science', 'Why this happens in the arts', and we talk in those particular terms. As parents we have always got fed up with our children saying to us, 'Why does this work in this way?' 'Why Daddy? Why?' But we want a society, and children who leave school at the age of sixteen asking that 'Why' question all the time. That is what our educational objectives should be about.

I, therefore, see the arts playing a crucial part in any National provision of education. We have, I think, a number of other tasks ahead of us. I think we shall have to change parental perception to a certain extent and that is a challenge for all of us. We have a real danger ahead of us that parents somehow see the sciences, maths, technology, as the hard road to a job. But that what goes on in the arts is seen as soft and is irrelevant. We do not share that view and those of you who teach do not share that view. What we need to do is to make sure that we all recognise and persuade parents of the value of what goes on in the arts because they make an essential contribution towards the individual child. We also have to persuade Government that there is a need for additional training for teachers in the arts subjects. There must be more in-service training, and there must be a commitment in that respect and that means that the arts have to be a central part of what goes on in the schools.

Can I also raise one additional item that concerns us greatly, and that is, whilst the Government says it is in the process of clarifying the law, they have published a consultative document on educational charges. That document I feel, to many Local Authorities up and down the country, will not be seen as a clarification process but will be seen as a green light, and that green light will lead to charges in areas that will be very important for the arts. It will be the visit to the theatre, it will be the visit to the museum, and I feel that many of us have failed to address a related matter there. My own younger son has just started his GCSE options. He is, incidentally, totally uncatered for in terms of the National Curriculum. I have to confess this, maybe I ought to confess to the Minister about him at a later stage, but he is doing information technology. That is because I told him at one stage that Kenneth Baker was the information technology Minister before he became Secretary of State. It really is a great shock for a youngster at the age of fourteen to then find that the information technology Minister, when he became Secretary of State, had written information technology out of the National Curriculum. So we got over that shock. His other great desire was to do drama as a GCSE Subject. I had to then suggest to him that it may be a little bit difficult but as you are fourteen you will get away with it before the National Curriculum comes in. So I have one of the most artistic computer operators in the business at home!

But that sort of flexibility, I think, is crucially important and is part of educational philosophy as well, but when it came to making those choices with him at the age of fourteen for GCSE, two points struck me. One is that at the age of fourteen, youngsters want to make choices for themselves, they are mature and feel they are mature and I do worry a little bit about the philosophy that panders to them and says we know what is best. You do not know what is right for you at the age of fourteen. And secondly, that there is, I think, the need to address an educational argument which says that certain things like bad medicine are good for you, but things you enjoy are not necessarily good for you. I have always had a very simple view of life. Those things I enjoy doing I believe I might do well. Those things I do not enjoy doing I never actually perform tremendously well, and I do not want to see an educational system where we drive youngsters into slots because nasty medicine will make them grow up. All evidence previously suggests that nasty medicine doesn't work in that respect.

I digress here for a moment in relation to my son's GCSE choices. A number of those options already involve charges on us as parents for various activities: a trip to the theatre, a field study for geography. Maybe we ought to address the cost of the GCSE exam for parents because a lot of parents are going to find it extremely difficult. Whilst it is the right exam, maybe politically we have to look at the ways in which parents are going to find the strain, because it was £3.00 for a theatre trip. That is a lot of money for a lot of parents and we have to take that on board.

I'll finish though by simply repeating what I have already said. That I very strongly hold a view of education that it must be broad, it must be liberal, it must be liberated and it must create a culture and climate of attainment. The arts in all their forms play a central part in that. Phoenix Dance and Northern Contemporary Dance are reference points for me and I hope we can keep them at the top of the agenda and as key reference points in this debate.

KEITH SWANWICK, INSTITUTE OF EDUCATION, UNIVERSITY OF LONDON

The notes for this presentation were written on a word processor. One thing to be learned from such an activity is the concept of *menus*. A menu is, quite simply, what is possible at a particular level, what range of choice is feasible within the limitations of the menu. This metaphor may appear to be somewhat mechanical. This is misleading. I am trying to describe what is also a biological and psychological truth. Every organism does what it can, it has a margin of manoeuvre. Fresh water plankton can do very little, but they *can* waft themselves up and down in rivers and thus get carried into different temperatures and current speeds, maximising their chances of survival.

In this way the Secretary of State does what he can in his environment - he moves up and down within the deepening stream of the National Curriculum. We have to decide how to respond depending on the menus in which we find ourselves and our powers of mobility.

Many of us also see the value of having a more articulated and publicly declared policy on the school curriculum: a move away from the arbitrary; away from the idiosyncrasies of individual schools and teachers; away from the undeclared and hidden consensus and the shaping of curriculum by examination boards.

There may be new opportunities - new menus - in which we can operate, new streams in which arts educators might swim. Be clear though, not all is new by any means.

The Course should provide for instruction in the English Language and Literature, at least one language other than English, geography, history, mathematics, science and drawing, with due provision for manual work and physical exercises, and, in a girls' school for Housewifery. Not less than 4 hours per week must be allotted to English, geography and history, not less than 3 hours to the language where only one is taken or less than 6 hours where two are taken; and not less than 7 hours to science and mathematics, of which at least 3 must be for science. The instruction in science must be both theoretical and practical. (*1904 Regulations for Secondary Schools*)

This does not appear to be so very different from The National Curriculum 5 - 16, July 1987. Nor is it very different from the 'status quo' curriculum of most schools today, except for less emphasis on technology and (later on in the document) a strong reference to Latin. The arts maintain a lower profile in the official pronouncement of 1904 than is presently the case in 1987, except for English Literature which, one suspects, rides on the back of the more utilitarian functions of language. The spread of subjects, allocated time, concern for 'standards' and the marginality of the arts has shifted little in 84 years. Let me try to identify what I think is significant for us in the consultation document *The*

National Curriculum 5 - 16. The main feature is that the proposals appear to be collections of apparently commonsense educational beliefs. Each belief though, arises from a particular view of education, a theoretical template, or metaphor. The doctrines from which these intentions arise are not self-evident truths. On the contrary, they are essentially theories which, it is assumed, are tenable and might be backed up and tested by evidence of some kind. I know that the Secretary of State is not alone in Britain in taking up a currently fashionable anti-intellectual stance. To describe the proposals as essentially theoretical may therefore be uncongenial. The plain truth is though, that no human mind is free from the impulse towards theorising, any more than human physiology can get by without breathing. So let us resist theories that complain about theorising, as though it were an unnecessary and expensive waste of time. Secretaries of State for Education, DES Inspectors, LEA Advisers and teachers all theorise, well or badly as the case may be. Take the present preoccupation with testing for example. The concepts of criterion referencing, and of summative assessment, now so widely used by all our colleagues in education, and the long-established (though controversial) concept of objectives were not generated in Westminster, at the DES or in Education Authorities, but in universities and colleges. In music education, for instance, the influential definitions of composition, performance, audition and of expressive character and structural elements that can, for example, be found (without references) in the National Criteria for GCSE and in HMI documents, did not materialise out of thin air but were given substance by the research of academics, your new chairman for one. It is undeniable that theoretical concepts filter into and influenced practice. Lively and critical theorising is one defence we have against the arbitrary, the subjective, the dogmatic and the doctrinaire; it is the way on which, as Karl Popper says, we can transcend ourselves. There is nothing so practical as a good theory and so much of a hindrance as a bad one.

Here, it seems to me, are some of the crucial theoretical pictures that are projected onto the future of British education in *The National Curriculum 5 to 16.*

1. Acceptance of an objectives model of the curriculum

Phrases like 'setting clear objectives' and having realistic 'expectations' along with the idea of 'attainment targets', communicate the sense of a curriculum 'out there', something precise and objective, as real as the milk bottle on the doorstep. Indeed, the curious phrase inherited from Sir Keith Joseph, 'the delivery of the curriculum', carries with it just that image of the milk float with its neatly stacked bottles and cartons; the product measured out precisely; labelled blue or gold top; sterilised yet nourishing, delivered. Let us be clear what this means for classroom transactions in general: teachers are to know in advance what learning outcomes are to be brought about; they are to devise activities to ensure that pupils achieve them; they are to have ways of assessing the level of this achievement. Objectives are to do with prediction, knowing in advance where we are going. The theoretical template of industrial production, conceiving of education as though it were a process of manufacturing pre-specified objects, lies behind this curriculum perspective.

There is, of course, a literature that contests this view of education as inadequate to match the reality of learning processes in general and classroom transactions in particular. I shall not rehearse the arguments of Stenhouse or Eisner here, but merely note that teaching to pre-specified objectives may produce work-to-rule-attitudes, can sometimes de-motivate students and can inhibit problem-solving and creative work. Working on a conveyor belt may be necessary but it is not likely by itself to equip pupils 'for the challenges of employment in tomorrow's world', a world where independence of thought and the ability to see new possibilities may be more important than meeting other

2. There is to be substantially more testing

We are told that having 'attainment targets' is 'a proven and essential way towards raising standards of achievement'. (No references for this proof!) These targets will be the standards used for assessment and 'at the heart of the assessment process there will be nationally prescribed tests' which will supplement individual teachers' assessments. Clearly, much time and money is going to be spent on testing; resources which, presumably, should will be diverted from teaching. Testing is thought to be essential, both in the interests of quality control, which is important for the consumer (the nation generally and parents in particular?), and as a spur to the labour force (teachers and students?). The metaphor of *accountancy* is at work here.

We know what is likely to happen here in the real world of school. Teachers will teach towards the tests, especially under conditions of appraisal. But are tests always the best method of assessment? Would a test be a realistic technique for assessing E.M. Forster's ability as a novelist, Rembrandt as a painter or Ravi Shankir as a musician or Rutherford as a scientist? Are tests always suitable for assessing childrens' ability to write cogently, to speak convincingly, to design, draw, paint, sing, play and dance?

3. And how is all this to be effected?

The main agents of curriculum generation and scrutiny are to be the Secretary of State, the DES Inspectors, a National Curriculum Council, a School Examinations and Assessment Council and Subject Working Groups. A Task Group on Assessment and Testing is also envisaged and LEA's have a role to see that statutory functions have been performed. Between them, these bodies will thrash out the structure, content of the curriculum and the assessment of pupils. The technique here is that of belt and braces. The curriculum is too important to be left to chance. Nails and screws are to be used along with rivets and glue. Nothing must fall apart: the emperor will have trousers and they will not be allowed to fall down. One fears that such a piecemeal structure will make for confusion and muddle.

4. What specifically about the Arts in all this?

Unlike our position in the 1904 Regulations, in 1987 we do not entirely escape official notice. Art and music at least are amongst the 'foundation' subjects and it may be possible to sneak dance in with PE, has been suggested by the Minister of State, Angela Rumbold. Drama is most likely to be subsumed under English. Little is said specifically about primary schools but in secondary schools art, music, drama and design may be allocated around 10% of the total time which seems to come to about 35 minutes each every week. In the 4th and 5th years, these four subjects, it is suggested, might be combined and also take an additional 10% each if they are to be taken to GCSE. As for the testing programme at 7, 11, 14 and 16, the arts seem to be regarded differently from most other curriculum areas: there will only-be 'guidelines' rather than 'specific attainment targets'. There will though, be Subject Working Groups for music and art - drama seems to come in and out of focus and dance appears to be ignored altogether.

Teachers of the arts may well wonder why they have been let off the more radical testing programme, but suspect that this may be because the arts are not felt to be so important. We remind ourselves that the curriculum subjects that appear to lend themselves to testing, maths and science in particular, get more time and, as we know, more resources of all kinds. Within the timetable, the idea of half an hour each week strung out over several years is unappealing, enabling us to neither relate to children nor to initiate worthwhile activities. We might have to press for an uneven distribution of time over the years of schooling. Maybe other subject colleagues would rather have substantial immersion in a subject over a shorter total period than dribble time away in unsuitably brief snatches. Do we have any room for manoeuvre?

Just like the Secretary of State, arts educators appear less than clear about what they are up to. Are the arts important human activities or aren't they? Can they be tested or can't they? Is there something to learn and therefore to teach or isn't there? If there is something to learn, can we see when it has been learned or is the learning invisible? Many arts teachers feel great sympathy with Michael Polanyi when he says - a classic formulation this - 'we can know more than we can tell'. His concept of tacit knowledge is totally opposed to the idea of pre-specified and observable learning and therefore is set against the idea of measurable objectives. If we can't see it, how can we measure it? And it is often said that judgments of any kind, let alone measurement by testing, is particularly difficult in the arts. After all, look at the fools that critics of the arts frequently make of themselves. Posterity knows better perhaps? Instant judgments can be silly. At this point it seems to me that we can go in two quite different directions. We can say, 'with the arts you can never tell, you can't be sure, its all rather subjective, we all are trying to resolve different 'sensate problems' in arts activities (cf. Ross and Witkin) If so, then assessment of any kind, let alone the narrow view of assessment as merely testing, becomes anathema - accursed. I regard this as not only politically foolish, but worse, untrue. Such an attitude invalidates the whole idea of education in the arts. How can we teach what we do not understand? How can we respond to students in any meaningful way without assessing? To teach is to assess, to weigh up, to appraise, in order more adequately to respond. The alternative view is to acknowledge that it might very well be possible to assess artistic work more reliably and consistently, certainly the work of most children - leaving aside more problematic geniuses - but we appear to lack confidence at present. More reliable assessment in the arts will be needed, not only for formative purposes in classrooms but also to meet the inevitable pressure towards making such judgments public. Let us confess: we do not yet know how best to assess the artistic, musical, dramatic, poetical and dance work of pupils. But we are not entirely helpless in this matter and when we get together to talk carefully about how to assess the work of pupils and how to respond to their work, we tend more to agreement than strife. Just because it is not yet possible to be totally confident in this sphere does not mean that this is necessarily always going to be the case. Take, for instance, the phenomenon of radiation. Radiation has always existed and had its effects on human life, and yet has only very recently become measurable, I want to suggest that the arts assessment has just not yet received sufficient research attention for us to feel secure in our judgments. What a repulsive thing to say! Surely the arts are the last bastion against explanation, a mysterious area of ritual, a domain of magic, impossible to analyse without destroying the sacred mystery of 'wholeness' and 'impenetrable depths', that special light which gives to human living a special quality, causing us to glow more brightly. Let me ask the question: has research into radiation prevented anyone from acquiring a sun-tan? Understanding how the arts function and how people develop in their capacities to make art and respond to art can only illuminate teaching and infuse quality into curriculum practice and such understanding may enrich our experience of the arts, though it can never substitute for this experience. I am really talking about the development of critical discourse, the idea of education as 'criticism'.

The central problem

Fundamentally, the documentation on the National Curriculum lacks vision, vision of tomorrow's world as well as a vision of how today's world might be a richer place. Schools to be conceived of as factories for the production of learning; the products of which are to be predetermined by committees and quality-controlled by tests which may turn out to be no more than paper and pencil exercises bearing little relationship to the real world of artists, musician, painters and designers; dancers, writers, actors and playwrights? Are the metaphors of the factory, the accounts department and the safety of belt and braces really powerful enough to lift the quality of education in anything, let alone the arts? I fear not, and offer an alternative picture. Schools function not in one way but in two. Firstly, they are certainly places in which learning should take place. Some of this learning is predictable and therefore can be planned in a fairly sequential way, putting down markers for achievement and identifying the stages that most pupils might follow in order to achieve. We shall also try to be sensitive to alternative learning outcomes, those valuable steps forward which were not predicated by national committees but which may make all the difference to the special character of each individual.

The model of the factory is of standardised production: the model of the arts is what is new and fresh, what is unique. We too, shall also be looking for 'excellence', trying to have pupils travel far down many roads, hoping that they will make the future.

Secondly, we shall be, along with our students, part of the shaping and reshaping of a community. A school is a social organism, not a machine. The quality of the life of this organism depends on many things; but colour and line, gesture and movement, dance and song, ceremony and ritual, are among the elements that sustain the life of human societies and, while tending towards a communal sense, perhaps even a feeling of 'oneness', also throw us back on ourselves, causing us to reappraise ourselves, our relationships and the values of the community in which we find ourselves.

The arts are an essential part of the fabric of living. No cohesive community exists without recourse to the range of symbolic discourse we call the arts. They must also be part of the fabric of schools, if schools are to be places where motivation is present, where great traditions are respected and entered into, where human values are celebrated.

The arts may be taught in classrooms but they are more frequently learned in action, through participation in events, in celebrations, in the enhancement of the physical and psychological environment. We should recognise that the school timetable cannot contain the school curriculum, though maybe it should contain more than it does. The issue of 'directed time' and arts accessibility will have to be squarely faced, unless we want schools to be grey, dry institutions - hardly a satisfactory preparation for 'tomorrow's world'.

Saying this does not absolve us from a good deal of hard work, including hard thinking and careful and systematic observation of what children actually do and can do in the arts. This is the place in the river where we, members of NAEA, like the plankton, have to be swimming up and down to find helpful currents. We need to work together towards more sensitive and helpful assessment of children's work, generating a decent theory which describes, explains and starts to predict artistic development, though never the outcome of any particular art project - that would violate the enterprise. This is necessary, not because it has is required by our other people but because it is essential for the quality of our own work as teachers. Testing as such will never be of much if any value to us. We ought though, to be able to sustain an alternative vision of assessment as criticism, criticism of the folio, the poem, the dance, the improvisation, the performance, the composition, the design, the artifact - objects and events from the real world.

When I say that the 'Red Book' lacks vision, I mean, among other things that it fails to motivate, to inspire us. There is a lack of literary quality in this plodding prose which compares badly with another official document from 1904, the *Elementary Code*. A brief passage may illustrate this.

The purpose of the Public Elementary School is to form and strengthen the character and to develop the intelligence of the children entrusted to it, and to make the best use of the school years available, in assisting both girls and boys, according to their different needs, to fit themselves, practically as well as intellectually, for the work of life.

For the *work of life*, not the *life of work*! This telling phrase captures an important difference of emphasis. Such a resonance lingers in the mind and still has the power to permeate educational transactions in today's world.

DAVID HARGREAVES, CHIEF INSPECTOR, ILEA

Perhaps I could begin by addressing the matter of the National Curriculum and by reminding colleagues that there is a commitment to the National Curriculum, of the concept of a National Curriculum, from both the Conservative and the Labour parties. I do not know whether you agree or not with the National Curriculum. I do, and for me the good news of the Red document is simply this, that part of the document sets out a number of purposes and intentions lying behind the National Curriculum that I think, if written by the Labour Party, would look very little different. I myself agree with the vast majority of these purposes and intentions and I suspect that you do too. If we quibble, we quibble with detail. The controversy comes in relation to the means by which these broad intentions might be realised, but at the end is the good news, that at least there is common ground with the Government about many of the purposes and intentions.

There is more good news that at least some of the arts subjects will be compulsory for all, throughout their years of schooling to the age of 16, and I say that this is good news because I can guarantee that I can take you to Secondary Schools in any of our many Local Authorities and find quite a number of children who are taking either no arts subjects in the fourth and fifth year or perhaps at best one or two superficial periods a week and I, for a long time, and I guess you too, have preached against this. I was slightly alarmed by Mr Fatchett, this morning, celebrating choice for young people. Not that I am against choice, but if you push it, and I do not think he intended to, if you push choice heavily in the fourth and fifth year you are back to the elaborate options schemes which we have dealt with in the past, and you have to face the fact that some children will choose to take no arts at all. Is that defensible? I think not. So there is some good news that at least the arts, or part of them, are fully in and they become part of the entitlement of every child throughout the period of compulsory schooling and in that we should rejoice.

But what about the bad news? The bad news is that the thinking in the document about the arts is very primitive. Ten percent of time is too little and the proposals are incomplete - the relative absence of dance, film studies, media studies and so on. Now let us look at these. The thinking is simply in terms of traditional subjects and I absolutely agree with Derek Fatchett this morning, when he said that one would have expected more to be said about process. I do not, however, think that in practice, you would have expected a document like this to have described the Curriculum in terms of process. It is true that our thinking has advanced very considerably in recent years on process versus content, but the truth is that most school timetables or a least secondary school timetables are still constructed in terms of subjects and indeed teachers themselves are structured into subject departments.

The trouble is that this is a document for fives to sixteens and you would never guess from the *Red Book* that primary schools think about the Curriculum in very different ways. That is not simply to put an absolute blessing on our primary education colleagues. A lot of primary school teachers and their heads in fact find it quite difficult to describe, account for and calculate what children are doing in relation to particular curriculum areas. It is not a easy problem for them. But you certainly would not guess from the *Red Book* that in both Primary and Secondary sectors in recent years many colleagues have been developing exciting cross curricular and modular courses which seem to fall very much outside the scope of the *Red Book*. It is perhaps as a result of this poor, primitive thinking that Art and Music are named as the Foundation subjects and Drama only appears in the fourth and fifth year illustration and Dance is not mentioned at all. I found it somewhat disingenuous this morning for the minister of State to say that Dance was really in. I agree with her that the exciting growth of CDT, in recent years acts as a potential bridge between Mathematics, Science and Technology onto the small island of the arts and that is not the kind of bridge that many of us conceived for CDT. Ten percent is, of course, to little time for the arts in the fourth and fifth year. You have to remember that you have only got about ten percent for all the rest of the options, and since ten percent is the minimum that is required for a public examination then if you look at the one area of schooling where the illustration is given for fourth and fifth year, you get the impression that the Government considers that no child should be taking more than one examination subject in the arts excluding English. The alternative would be to take more than one subject in some kind of combined arts course. Not I do not use the word 'integrated'; some kind of combined arts course. The trouble is, our experience in combined arts courses for public examination is still extremely limited and under-developed, so they are not ready to fit into such a scheme. The alternative, as Keith Swanwick implied, is that you take several arts, but you take none of them as a public examination. In other words, as far as the arts are concerned in the fourth and fifth year of secondary school it is possible to achieve breadth but apparently no depth! This would produce enormous problems for talented children who are perfectly capable of taking several public examinations in the arts, and it does appear to me that the arts area suffers here in comparison with Mathematics, Science and Technology. In other words the claim that the curriculum is balances is mistaken.

How do we solve this problem that has been posed for us by the Government? This is what we try to cram into the curriculum. The Scots have expressed this very well - they described the curriculum as a bookshelf and it is a bookshelf that is full, many people want to add extra volumes but no one wants to take any of the existing volumes off the shelf. That was written in a Scottish report on Education, precisely forty years ago and think of the additional volumes we have been trying to put on since. I do not know what the solution to that is. The Government, I believe, should have been more open in saying that we are trying to cram too much in, and let us not pretend that most schools have solved that problem. We have to join in the discussion about what we put into the limited space and that means that we will have to consider possibilities that are tough. One, for instance, would be that there should not be both a language and a humanities subject on the curriculum with ten percent each. You could make more space for the arts by saying it should be either a Language or History or Geography. In other words, you reduce their time. Or you might say that there ought to be thirty percent languages and humanities, but it acts like a constrained option and pupils could take one of each if they wished, but they might be able to take two or one, one of the other and then nothing in the third area, so you could get two arts, one language, no humanities. Or you might want to argue, and I'll come back to this later, that we simply have to get more in by extending the day, in other words making more use of extended provision outside normal school hours. Some kind of solution is essential.

What worries me about the reaction of the profession to the red document is that there have been very few examples of alternative schemes offered by the profession. If is easy to knock down what they have suggested. It is much more testing to come back with an alternative. The alternatives do need to be brought forward because if the present scheme goes through unamended) then it seems to me that Music is guaranteed a place (and that is splendid) but it is likely to be that a minority take Music to the public examination and that might be made even more so if charges for instrumental music are introduced. The result of this, that Music is likely to be for a minority for public examination is that Art will gain enormously and have a very firm place on the Curriculum. Drama, despite what Angela Rumbold said, seems to me to be in imminent danger. I could very easily find itself eroded as Headteachers and Governing Bodies, under pressure to start the Curriculum, start to lose qualified Drama teachers. Drama could return to a subset of English just as Dance could be reduced to a subset of Physical Education. Dance is in the same position as Drama and I think that film and media studies could virtually disappear.

What I am left with is a strong belief that we have to generate some notion of balances arts to match the balanced sciences. It is incredible the progress that our science colleagues have made in winning ground not only in the profession but with parents and politicians for the concept of balanced science as an essential part of education. It is no longer a matter of simply talking in terms of Mathematics and Physics and Chemistry or as sciences, but generating a principle of balanced science for all. The battle for balanced arts is still to be won and if we could win that battle, much of the terrain that we are debating could look very different indeed. It would help us to get around the problems of carousels and so on which I think be-devil much arts education in our schools, because carousels in themselves have not come to terms with the notion of balanced arts education.

Now, Angela Rumbold reaffirmed that the government would not dictate the percentage to be allocated to subjects in the legislation, and it is very welcome to have that reaffirmation. I fear, however, that it is somewhat disingenous. It is, or course, only an illustration that is provided in the Red Book. I fear, however, that the illustration will remain in the minds of many. It will remain in the minds of parents and it will remain in the minds of Headteachers and Governing Bodies and the problem of time allocation will not go away. It has to be addressed, and I fear that many will address it in terms of the illustration, and that the Government will be in the privileged position of being able to distance itself from the illustration and say that we have decided it. The place of any Curriculum area in the battle for resources and timetable space may, in practice, be determined not just by the illustration, but by the testing programme. If this happens in the fourth and fifth year of our secondary schools it will have massive implications for what happens in the earlier years not only of secondary but also of primary schooling.

But let us turn to testing and like Keith Swanwick I want to look closely at paragraph twenty-four of the *Red Book*, because it says there will be guidelines for Art and Music (and, I may say, Physical Education) rather than the attainment targets which will apply to English, Mathematics and Science and it is expected, but it is a little bit unclear, to languages and the humanities.

What is the implication? I take the implication to be that there will be no National testing for arts subjects and what is one's reaction to that?

Well, at first it is a blessed relief. Assessment is notoriously difficult in the arts. We are making progress, but we have a long way to go. But crude testing would set us back a long way. But the other side of that relief, that we may not be subjected to National Testing, leads me to fear that one will be marginalised. Public opinion could rapidly move to the position, once the National Curriculum and testing are implemented, that if it is not tested it is unimportant and if people believe it, and Headteachers believe it, there is an enormous threat to the time allocation to the arts and, therefore, to the staffing - in particular to Drama and Dance.

A second consequence for the lack of testing for the arts is the impact on the perception, not only of what is important to the Curriculum but also what counts as achievement. Some of you will know that when some colleagues and I were involved in writing, 'Improving Secondary Schools', for Inner London, we emphasised that the growth of the comprehensive school had really brought us into line with a good deal of primary education in widening the concept of achievement, away from the narrow focus of the grammar school on the memorisation of propositional knowledge. We have talked about the four aspects of achievement, and aspect two was practical knowledge and aspect three was a range of personal and social skills, including 'learning to work alone without supervision', but also including, 'the capacity to co-operate in teams with other people', and we see aspects two and three now have to have a rightful place in the secondary school as they have in the best primary schools. When we drafted that section, which was perhaps the most important and influential piece of our report, we had in mind, or certainly I had in mind, as exemplars of a balance of the four aspects of achievement, the teaching of the arts. They know, and have known for a long time, the importance of aspects two and three and I have to say that in the ILEA we probably have more that our fair share of high quality teaching of the arts. But aspects two and three are difficult to assess. It is not impossible, but it is difficult, and if I see testing as one sort of assessment, I am quite sure that aspects two and three are more difficult to test than aspect one, memorising propositional knowledge, and the danger, therefore, is that those subjects of the arts which best exemplify the four aspects of achievement will not be subject to testing the whole of the exciting developments in recent years towards broader conception of assessment could be reduced.

The irony is, that I find my colleagues in Mathematics, Science and Technology are themselves changing their conceptions of testing and achievement. Some of the most exciting things that have developed in Mathematics and Science and CDT in recent years has been the growth of graded assessment schemes. They began talking about graded tests, but within a year they were talking about graded assessments. It was a massive conceptual shift. It would be tragic if that too were to be thrown away. Much will depend, of course, on Professor Black's task group on assessment and testing and on the working groups in Mathematics and Science. They will pave the way for the relation of testing to assessment in general.

I also note, as Keith Swanwick does, that the arts get guidelines but they get the guidelines *last* apparently. If you look through the relevant paragraph, you will see that the subject working groups will be established in the following order: Mathematics and Science - already in operation, English will follow next, then we go to Modern Languages, then we go to Technology and it will pick up what is going on in Mathematics and Science and then we come to History and Geography. In this critical paragraph the arts strangely are not even mentioned. The implication is that the guidelines on the arts will come very late. My suspicion is that this reflects the Government thinking about the importance of the arts. But the other side of that coin may well be a virtue from the Association's point of view. There is time to reflect and influence events if you choose to exercise that influence.

There was a most fascinating article by Malcolm Ross in the TES, a few weeks ago and I am sorry that he is not here, as it were to present that message to you himself. I hope you saw it, it was a very short article on page two, it takes a few minutes to read, it was a swashbuckling piece, it was a war cry. For Malcolm, the *Red Book* represents the end of the line, the logical culmination of a systematic attach on the heart of education. It is a war cry because he believes this is the point where teachers and Arts teachers in particular have to take a stand. The have, he said, set about destabilising the Secretary of State and all his works. Well, you will make you own judgment, no doubt, on whether you think Malcolm is right. But it seems to me that if the teaching profession has learnt anything in the last two or three years, one of the lessons it ought to have learned is that blunt opposition to Conservative Secretaries of State tends to lead Secretaries of State not only to win most of the battles but the whole war and I do not believe in Malcolm's war cry. I think that arts educators are now in a position of having to be not only as gentle as doves but as wise as serpents. You will have to be strategic. Blatant opposition will fail. It will merely convince the Government of what a hopeless lot you are and why they needed to intervene.

How, therefore, do I think you need to be strategic? Let me make four suggestions to your Association. First be positive. Recognise that you do have some common ground and I think you learnt from Angela Rumbold this morning, there is more common ground with Ministers that you may have thought from the *Red Book*. But that means not so much a war cry, but the development of powerful arguments. I think you should argue your case rigorously and with all the vigour you can muster, but also with all the intellect and skill that you can muster too. Look for the strengths of the National Curriculum and build on the platforms that are there to build upon. Secondly I would say make concrete arguments not rhetoric. Rhetoric makes the arts troops feel good but it doesn't win you many friends outside. So they have to be sharp and concrete arguments and you have got to say, if you want more space and time for the arts, what you would be willing to displace or how you would argue it and how you would organise it. Thirdly, be 'creative' in your arguments. If you, of all groups of teachers, cannot be creative in your arguments, heaven help the rest. 'Creative' to me has always meant a special combination of discipline and imagination. I believe myself that the most important way in which you can be creative is to provide some detailed arguments about balanced arts to match the balances sciences, but I believe there may be other ways in which you should allow your imaginations to flourish.

Let me give you one example. If you take areas like Dance or Media Studies they are already not as fully developed as they might be. If you accept that many of our relatively small comprehensive schools even at present find it difficult to offer the full range of arts courses to young people, then you may be led to the view that there may need in every Local Authority to be at least some schools which are prepared to offer some form of extended provision, a wider provision to those that undertake it. There are young people who will want more arts education than average and to that degree there ought to be a choice. There ought to be a minimum level of arts for all but there ought to be some children who do way beyond the minimum. I do not believe that most of our schools can currently provide that. But it also means, too, that if we are going to preserve some subjects like Dance and build upon them, we may have to have much more imaginative ways of making provision for them, we may have to think of teachers who have appointments in one or more institutions which is still not a common way of solving that problem. But you have the capacity of being creative. You have the capacity to put forward the alternatives which the Government will want to listen to. The Government, I believe, does not want simply to listen to criticism, however well founded, and well intentioned. It is a political reality that you must offer constructive alternatives for them to consider. My fourth and final piece of advice interestingly tunes in I think, where Keith Swanwick ended. It is, act together. The trouble is that teachers of the arts are so often merely a loose confederation of subject specialist interests. You have not sufficient experience of acting together, your track record is poor.

Let me compare this Association with the Association of Science Education. I do not know how many of you have been to their annual conference, but it is quite an experience. It is on American convention scale. Thousands, thousands of people go. They have all the publishers and all of the resources across the whole of science teaching available, every major publisher goes, every examination board goes to those annual conferences. There are hundreds of lectures. The programme is the thickness of a book. They not only have things on science education for teachers but they bring in large numbers of distinguished scientists and industrialists to make presentations. Large numbers of firms arrive and put up stands. You cannot be bored at an ASE Conference. You are spoilt for choice by the multiple papers that are being presented and you can spend at least a day going around the publishers and firms stalls to see what they have got to offer. You go to the ASE with an empty suitcase and bring it back full. In the ILEA we send unusually large numbers of teachers to the ASE because my science inspector colleagues tell me it is one of the most effective in-service courses in science that exists.

Where is the equivalent in the arts? Why shouldn't you have something like that? It seems to me that in this Association you have got the embryo of an equivalent for the arts. The ASE has brought science teachers together and it has changed their conceptions of science teaching but it has also influenced a lot of important people who are interested in science education but are not part of it and they have friends outside education.

We have learnt since Jim Callaghan's speech (which I didn't realise was disallowed by the Labour Party), we have learnt since then that most politicians have taken, and I suspect still do take the view that education is far too important to be left to the teachers. That age has gone. Let us be realistic and face up to it. The alternative is not for us to be ashamed of what we do but to go out and win friends and influence people.

I think the arts have moved on immensely in the last decade, I am very impressed by so many of the people I meet both in what they say and what they have achieved. I am proud of the progress we are making in ILEA and I suspect that those of you from other authorities would share the same sense of pride. I am thrilled at the success of SCDC's Arts in Schools Project so ably led by Ken Robinson and the fact that we are meeting at all today suggests that we believe that there is much to do.

I am very grateful to you for the privilege of being here to share my thoughts with you. I wish you courage to face the hard work that I believe lies ahead of you, the rewards are potentially huge.

PART TWO

ASSESSMENT AND THE ARTS CURRICULUM

One of the crucial areas at present is that of assessment. Assessment in the arts is always a controversial matter and there is a range of opinion from those who say that there should be no form of assessment at all to those who believe that what can be taught can be assessed and that the arts fall to some extent within a category of what can indeed be taught.

There are no easy answers to this question. Though we have an opportunity to clarify our thinking about the arts in the curriculum through the lens of assessment by putting to scrutiny the processes by which we judge the work of children and others, we inevitably raise the whole question of what it means to be a critic in the arts. For whatever purpose assessment may be used, whether to help in the day-to-day business of teaching or to provide a formal qualification, judgments about the qualities of artistic products and events must colour all learning-teaching transactions.

The following papers represent a range of perspectives on assessment and the arts.

THE PROBLEM OF AESTHETIC EDUCATION

PROFESSOR DAVID ASPIN, KINGS COLLEGE, UNIVERSITY OF LONDON

In January 1982 there was published the Report of a Committee set up by the Calouste Gulbenkian Foundation to study principles, practice and provision for the arts in educational institutions. In *The Arts in Schools*[1] we were concerned to put forward evidence and arguments that would convince those responsible for the framing and implementing of policies and programmes of instruction in our schools and colleges that would support the introduction to the activities of the arts subjects as a part of the curriculum for all pupils in them. Our principal motivation was to get the arts (music, dance, drama, fine art, poetry and so on) accepted as part of the 'core curriculum' in all schools; our case was presented to educational decision-makers at every level and in every sector, from head teachers to LEA advisers and inspectors, to chief education officers to the Secretary of State for Education himself.

The soundness of those arguments and the persuasiveness of the case we mounted can now be clearly discerned. Two years after the publication of The Arts in Schools (1982) we may justifiably claim that the theoretical argument about the place of the arts on the curriculum has been won. For in a speech to the North of England Education Conference in Sheffield on 6th January 1984, Sir Keith Joseph gave open support to one of the principal contentions of the case we advanced for the arts in schools:[2]

> the various elements of the curriculum need to be balanced in such a way as to optimise the contribution that each can make to the total education of the pupil. Insofar as each main element does something for the pupil that no other element does, or does as well, no pupil should miss the chance of getting out of each element the special competence and understanding which it helps him to acquire.

In a subsequent letter to the Chairman of the new School Curriculum Development Committee, Professor R. Blin-Stoyle, on 3rd February 1984, Sir Keith set out in further detail his views on priorities for curriculum development. His priority areas are English Language, mathematics, science and technology and the humanities. This last is the important point: aesthetic education is now maintained to be an educational priority by the Secretary of State.

Shortly after the appearance of Sir Keith's views there was published the Report of the Committee of the ILEA under the chairmanship of Dr D.H. Hargreaves on future strategies for secondary schools in London, *Improving Secondary Schools*.[3] In a section of that Report entitled 'The whole curriculum' (Section 3.4) the Committee make it clear that they accept and endorse the cases made out for the centrality of an aesthetic element in the core curriculum in a wide range of 'official' publications on the curriculum in recent years. They come to the importance of the arts in the later parts of the life of a pupil in school in the set of options related to a 'core' that they propose for years four and five:

> We believe that a pupil who could select a course of study in the fourth and fifth years which contained no aesthetic subjects at all would be following an unbalanced curriculum. We recommend that in the fourth and fifth years the creative arts should be grouped together as a constrained option from which every pupil must select at least one aesthetic subject In spite of current achievements there is, we believe, evidence of underachievement in the aesthetic domain amongst some pupils: this creative, aesthetic potential cannot be allowed to go untapped. (Section 3.9.22)

The Committee hoped that the implementation of this recommendation would go far towards countering danger for the arts, the inclusion of a reference to which must be ominous for all who are concerned to defend the continued presence of the arts in the 'core curriculum':

> At a time of falling rolls the aesthetic subjects, which are sometimes allocated 'low status' by some teachers and parents, are particularly vulnerable.

The situation described in the HMI *Secondary Survey*[4] is thus still with us: the arts are a prime example of those subjects that are regarded as 'frills' on the edge of serious and worthwhile curricula. The subjects thought by many parents and teachers to be fundamentals are still English, mathematics and the sciences, perhaps with a modern language added to this central core. These are the subjects that have 'high status': they are worlds of empirics and logic solely. For them any connection of the idea of objectivity with normative discourse would rest on a misconception concerning the typical features of each of these domains.

There has been sufficient work in the philosophy of science in recent years however to suggest that the separation proposed by positivists between the objective world of impersonal empirical data and the subjective world of personal idiosyncratic response rests upon epistemic foundations that are far from secure. Indeed it would be too much to say that, as a result of the objections to inductivism and positivism mounted variously by Popper, Kuhn, Lakatos and Feyerabend,[5] the world-picture embodied in the above separation must now be either abandoned or at least very substantially modified. As opposed to the notion that the sciences are value-neutral and theory-free, we may now maintain with some justification that our observation of phenomena is inescapably theory laden and our reflections upon them rooted in a complex network of human interests and concerns amongst which purposes and values will have their place. On this basis science is a species of theory construction, testing and refinement; on that basis too the admissibility of whole areas of investigation and intellectual interest, that had been previously rejected by positivists as 'subjective', to an expanded world of 'science' now becomes a matter for much more open discussion and adjudication. For now the concept of objectivity with which jealous guardians of the truths of science had made the criteria of warranted assertability in the empirical realm coercive upon the claims of candidates from all other realms for serious curriculum consideration has had to be changed.

There have been many versions of the concept of objectivity consequent upon the rebuttal of positivism by Popper and others. I wish to select only one from these and to concentrate upon the idea of objectivity as 'intelligibility'. And in talking of 'objectivity' in terms of 'intelligibility' I have two senses of 'intelligible' in mind here: the intelligibility of any form of public communication generally; and the way in which our appraisals of objects, persons, performances and products can be articulated and then justified. I am thus taking as my starting-point the notion of the intersubjectivity of the agreements and conventions that constitute the languages that we employ to communicate with each other about the world we share; I am not denying that there may be a private world of experience but I follow Wittgenstein here in maintaining that, for such experiences to have significance for other people, they must in some way or other be amenable to public inspection.[6] Further I use this point about the necessary public character of all linguistic interchange to claim that the vindication and defensibility of the judgments that we make concerning the value of some thing will be quite as 'objective' as any of the claims that we advance in other and different types of criticism, reflection and theorising. This will put the objectivity of our aesthetic judgments on a par with, though not necessarily in the same logical category as, the judgments we make in morals, history or indeed science and technology.

It is neither possible nor desirable for me to give some account or defence of the metaphysics of language, thought and world with which I am here proposing to work. A reading of some or all of the philosophers already cited would give that far better than I can. Let me simply adopt a figure from Ryle and place some pegs in the ground from which I want to try and draw out some strings of argument.[7] I state the following points as well-known theses which I wish to call in question and to maintain that, if we have any regard for them, it must be temporarily suspended for us to make any progress in the formation and elucidation of an account of objectivity and assessment in arts education, that will defend it from the criticisms that less well-disposed parents and teachers, politicians and industrialists may have mounted against them in the past. And in these criticisms such people may have been perhaps unconsciously aided and abetted by the very people who would be hostile to them in their attempts to marginalise that arts - the teachers themselves who continued overtly or tacitly to adhere to the myths that are inimical to and can be used to subvert a case for the arts in education.

These myths I believe should be abandoned or suspended:the view that there subsists a difference between the 'factual' world of the sciences and the 'values' world of the arts - between, in other words facts and values; between the world of intellect and that of feeling-between reason and emotion; between the world of hard work and disciplined learning on the one hand and that of spontaneity and creativity on the other; between the physical world and the spiritual world-between 'mind' and 'body'; and lastly between conception and articulation-between 'thought' and 'language'. The collapsing or at any rate the suspension of all these dualisms help us to approach the question giving some account of the objectivity of aesthetic judgments and showing how children's increasing ability and confidence in making them can be monitored and evaluated and I should like to take this suspension as my base for what follows.

I cannot however proceed without giving some preliminary indication of what I mean by 'language' for upon this notion much of what follows will depend. 'Language' I take to refer to those well-formed strings of noises, marks and signs articulated and capable in principle of being solid and respectable, not only, or so it is thought, because success in public examinations in them at 16+ confers access to employment, but also because they are 'hard' subjects in the sense that their content is held to be 'objective' and progress in them easily measured. Work in the arts - like much of moral religious and now political education - is often regarded as 'soft': it is suspect because subjective, unamenable to quantification and above all non-vocational.

If therefore the arts are to have priority in curriculum planning and development they will have to meet these charges. The importance of their doing so is underlined by the plans announced by Sir Keith Joseph in Sheffield for the attainment of his aim to raise standards in education. He proposed to do this in four ways.

to define the objectives of the main parts of the 5-16 curriculum so that everyone knows the level of attainment in each subject that should be achieved by pupils of different abilities at various stages in it;

to alter public examinations at 16+ so that they measure absolute rather than relative performance;

to establish the aim of bringing 80-90% of all pupils at least to the level now expected and achieved in 16+ examinations in individual subjects by pupils of average ability;

to do all this over a broad range of skills and competence in a number of subjects.

These then are demands to which the arts must endeavour to conform. For the arts evidently constitute the principal part of that aesthetic element in the curriculum upon which it is held to be reasonable to impose these requirements.

The question of the vocational or non-vocational nature of work in the arts in educational institutions has already been raised and, I believe answered in *The Arts in Schools* and I shall not give further attention to this matter here. What concerns me much more, in view of the above demands, are the issues of the objectivity of the arts, if any, and the possibility of making assessment of the skills, knowledge, values and attitudes that count as worthwhile outcomes of an education in them. The Sheffield speech requires arts teachers to specify attainments at various stages in pupil's progress and also to articulate their criteria for assessment. For only in this way, it is held, can such teachers measure up to the demand for accountability - the hidden agendum of so many parents and politicians at this time. And all this seems to me to turn on the question of whether in what sense if any the arts and the aesthetic judgments that issue in and from educational activity in them can be said to be objective.

Talk of 'objectivity' is of course not entirely unproblematic. There is a number of senses in which the word 'objective' can be employed. In the sense in which teachers and parents referred to in the foregoing paragraph employ it is typically applied to those areas of curriculum activity that have to do with 'facts' and 'evidence', where these are held to be established by the procedures of the natural sciences that cut down the role of the personal element in the observation and gathering of material by empirical means to an acceptable minimum of interference. This is the sense of objectivity employed by scientists of the positivist persuasion.

In contrast to the high degree of probability that the data-gathering instruments and methods of the empirical sciences assure are set the characteristics of individual taste and personal preference of subjects that many people attribute to our appraisal of art-objects. It is the thesis of the non-corrigibility of such appraisals and the notion of their being grounded in a person's psychological reactions and individual response that lead many to contrast them with the empirically-established corrigibility of scientific results and incontrovertible conclusions of such deductive system as mathematics and logic, the axioms of which are held to be paradigms of objectivity and impersonality. For such people 'objective' means 'provable by mathematical or scientific means'; subjective means 'reducible in the final analysis to personal preference and taste'. And with this goes often the corollary that, because such preferences are irredeemably private, they cannot be explained or justified; their status is ultimately that of prejudices, that self-evidently admit of no vindication, at least in educational terms.

'Objective' is used often in the case of the arguments that we might employ to support our judgment in matters of public policy, in the sense of their 'disinterestedness' or 'impartiality'. The supposed defensibility of such judgments lends them status of objectivity in the matter of the justification of our values of which Hume and later the emotivists are generally regarded as proponents. There is another way of taking this, however: there would be many who would deny objectivity to the domain of values and the justification of value-judgements entirely, and restrict it to the responded to as significance-bearing by another creature - language as the systematic and syntactic combination of symbolic signs for the purposes of communication.[8] Language has thus to do with the utterance, transmission and reception of meaning.

That only throws the problem of giving an account one stage further back: what is meant by 'meaning' in this sense! There are many ways in which this word can be used and an investigation into the meaning of meaning was attempted many years ago by Ogden and Richards in the book of that title.[9] G.H.R. Parkinson has rendered the problem of elucidating 'meaning' somewhat more tractable by distinguishing between some of the more common ways in which people employ the term.[10] 'Meaning' as 'value' ('his blessed allotment means everything to him') can be distinguished from meaning as 'intention' ('I mean to go to the cinema this evening'), from meaning as 'portent' ('rain before seven means fine before eleven'), from meaning as 'symbol' ('chien' in French means 'dog' in English). The sense in which we here are interested is however distinct again: it is the intelligibility of words, their semantic content and function, that is primary focus of interest for the philosopher of language. I can do little better than to quote Wittgenstein at this point:[11]

> For a large class of cases - though not for all - in which we employ the word 'meaning' it can be defined thus: the meaning of a word is its use in the language.

For some, therefore, there is no such 'thing' as the meaning of a word as some kind of entity existentially distinct from it; for them it is more sensible to follow the advice contained in the aphorism: 'Don't ask for the meaning; ask for the use'.

The meaning of an expression in language therefore is the account(s) that can be given of its place in interpersonal signification. Words can be clarified, responded to, paraphrased or translated, evaluated and assessed, discussed and argued over, developed and taken further. The meaning of an utterance in any form of discourse resides in its intelligibility, its capability of being elucidated, its evocative or emotive character, its assessability and its generative potential, *inter alia*. This account is by no means exhaustive nor is it meant to be: for some words are used in a variety of different ways, in different contexts and for different purposes. It is a characteristic of language that it changes over time and according to circumstance and thus to look for some one basic or essential, real meaning of expression would be to commit oneself to a search for a chimera. Curiously, however, that does not mean we can say what we like; there cannot be a 'Humpty-Dumpty' situation in our use of the noises, marks and signs we have learned to employ to communicate with our fellows about the world we share with them. Language is not idiosyncratic; indeed it is the long-established even if slowly-changing conventions of significance and sense in language that have enabled us, in a quite important way, to 'construct that world and to render it comprehensible and controllable. It is, taken in this way, the rules and conventions governing communication in language that stand as major touchstones for our perception of the world, that constitute, in their intersubjective agreements, the objective reality of the world we share. The languages that we speak are thus the guarantees of any sort of objectivity in the world of interpersonal communication; for they enable us to objectify our experience to it, to categorise it according to some sort of scheme and thus to try to reduce it to some sort of object capable of being appraised and understood.

It only remains for me to add that some of our linguistic articulations are not confined to our comprehensible in the discursive mode only; there are complex networks of significance and sense in the languages of posture, bodily movement, gesture and physiognomy that can only with great difficulty-even if at all - be set down or spoken words. It is possible, I am claiming for people to say things to each other of considerable complexity, sophistication and profundity, without ever opening the mouth. Certainly, if the language of love may serve as an example here, whole words of meaning can be conveyed by a look or a touch or a movement. And it is this consideration that gives us confidence in approaching the equally difficult and complex area of the understanding and assessment of meaning in the arts.

If we now have it conceded that there must be an aesthetic element in the compulsory curriculum in maintained schools we must be prepared to say how that element will along with the others, satisfy the Secretary of State's demands for breadth, balance, relevance and differentiation. Of these perhaps the last criterion is most critical for upon our version of it our answers to the other demands will in the final analysis depend. In what does the arts' (or 'our') peculiar claim to curriculum status depend? What are the features of educated judgments in the arts and aesthetics that are given by no other subject? what characteristics enable us to mark them off from sorts of knowledge and skills on which educational value might be placed? Some answers to these questions have already been essayed and it is not the purpose of this paper to endeavour to emulate the achievements of Strawson or Arnaud Reid in this respect. We may do sufficient to give such a differentiation by standing on their shoulders, so to speak, and give some such account of the typical features of informed aesthetic judgments as the following:[12]

1.   Aesthetic judgments are different from other types of discourse insofar as they are non-instrumental in character. Their value does not lie in the ways in which they promote the attainment of ulterior ends; rather it is to be found in the valued achievements that are internal to the activity of judging and making in the world of art.

2.   This means that artifacts will be such as to create satisfactions of various kinds in the contemplator of the artistic qualities they embody and re-present. I do not mean by this that the effects of works of art will be a function of their 'beauty' or some other such feature; for the effects of artifacts can be profoundly disturbing as a result of their stridency, ugliness, harshness or discord. All these are equally thought-provoking because of the effects that the disclosures of various artistic 'truths' that they promote bring about in the observer. These effects are excitements of one kind or another - like the effect Aristotle had in mind when he speaks of the cathartic effect of (or through) pity and fear that it was the task of the drama to bring about in the audience - and it is for that reason that I call them 'satisfactions'.

3.   These satisfactions will be such as can be experienced by someone standing in the role of a spectator. By this I mean that the making of aesthetic

judgment requires some conceptual distance between the one making the appraisal and the work being appraised; such an appraisal presupposes a stance apart in some way, even when one individual is involved. The artist who stands back and surveys the progress of his own work as he struggles to 'get it right' is necessarily adopting such a stance. Being a spectator or part of an audience involves bringing to bear upon a work quite a different sort of apparatus than that called for in the making of the work. That apparatus will be critical, an interpretive one, rather than constructive or creative.

4. Such interpretations or critiques will also be based upon the erection and application of a set of criteria of some sort. A work will be appraised by its judges operating from within some sort of theoretical perspective. It matters little whether we evaluate a novel in terms of its moral import, say, its honesty, integrity and authenticity, or its complexity of structure, its different textures, its subtle characterisation or its pace, whether we look at it as Leavisites or as structuralists. What is important here is that we are rating the work, within some class of comparison, as exhibiting a particular set of characteristics that count for us as normative in ratings within that class; these count as the benchmarks constituting excellence against which we measure the work. Aesthetic appraisals, in sum, presuppose some kind of theory of aesthetic value.

5. These theories will be those that have been proposed by cognoscenti - those who, on the basis of their own observation, interpretation and appraisal of works of art, will have come to some view as to what counts as artistic excellence generally for that class of artifact.

Their formulation and articulation will have been helped or hindered by the many counters, objections and amendments that people have variously proposed in their reaction to hearing such theories. This process of dialogue in turn rests on the intersubjective agreements that constitute the particular 'universe of discourse' to the rules and conventions of which talk in and about the arts has to conform if it is to be understood and accepted. This requires a community of discourses - a group of participants in a 'form of life' admission to which can only be secured by those who have such understanding and competence in the languages by which aesthetic meanings are communicated within that community. In a word, the ability to make aesthetic judgments comes directly from the ability to enter into the language-games in which approaches to the questions of value in our assessments of works of art are conceived, articulated and then understood. Of necessity then someone wishing to make such judgments of works of art will be one who has learned somehow to appreciate the different kinds of meaning in the world of aesthetics and the arts-performative, graphic, plastic, expressive, mimetic and the rest and to signify that appreciation in accordance with the canons of the logic determining warranted assertability in the field in question.[13]

To say what that meaning consists in is rather more difficult, however especially if we incline to the view that it is impossible, for good philosophical reasons, to give some unambiguous definition or clear conceptual analysis of 'aesthetic meaning'. Perhaps 'meaning as use' may give us some help here; We can look at works of art and examine both how other people react to them and the kind of account we might give of their effects on us. And in this endeavour we have the signal contributions of Arnaud Reid and Greger to aid us.[14]

Works of art 'speak to us' in some sense; of that there can be no doubt. But, like many other fine things in our world of thought and imagination, they contain many messages and the elucidation of their meaning is not rendered any easier by the consideration that the ways in which this meaning is embodied in a work of art and laid open to our reception and delection are not necessarily discursive in character. We are told that a friend of Schumann, on hearing him play a piece he had newly composed, asked him to explain it. 'Indeed, dear friend, I am anxious to explain it', said Schumann. 'It means this: ——, and he played it again. That is the point: if Schumann had been able to give a comprehensive verbal account of the 'meaning' of the piece he would have not needed to compose it in musical notation and play it in the way he did. There are whole words of meaning in *Guernica*, The *Ecstasy of St. Theresa*, or *The Tempest* but they are not such as Picasso, Bernini or Shakespeare could have written down fully in plain prose. That is the glory of such works but it is also a problem of understanding and appreciation for us; as Cicero remarked, 'every thing excellent is as difficult as it is rare'.

There is a further difficulty, too. Works of the art have, in some sense also, a 'life of their own'. They are organic, growing in richness, complexity and diversity as the time of their existence in the world passes. Just as *The Tempest* and the other works referred to have 'grown' over time and are now understood differently than when they were first 'published' to the world, so we can never come to the 'same work'. Heraclitus summed this up well: 'No man can ever step into the same river twice, for fresh waters are ever flowing down·upon him'.[15] The work itself acquires further life, strength and stature as a result of the increments to its store of meanings that generation upon generation of amateurs and interpreters and critics have added; while we ourselves acquire fresh stores of knowledge and insight that inevitably and inescapably bring us to work we have seen or heard before also in some sense as 'new persons'. It is one thing to come to a work for the first time; it is quite another to come to it again. But I suspect that the difference here is one degree, rather than kind, because of the fact that both we and the work are dynamically evolving organic entities.

We are also single 'beings'. A human being has many parts in one being, yet the totality is more than the mere sum of the parts. In this way each individual person is unitary and unique. So it is with work of art: it embodies many parts and a multiplicity of meanings in its single form of appearance, yet the whole is more than the sum of all these parts and meanings. That is what so fascinating and different about our contemplation of aesthetic objects: for the uniqueness of the works that we see as belonging to the aesthetic realm lies in the fact that they fuse, combine, synthesise and embody not only a complex of formal and material features and components but, crucially, an innumerable variety of meanings. Works of art are characterised by the way in which, to use Ehrenzweig's term, they 'de-differentiate' the various kinds of meaning: they combine and synergize whole 'layers' of intelligibility for us and present them to us for inspection and delight all embodied in one harmonious whole.[16] The activity and the difficulty of making aesthetic appraisals has to start being brought to bear upon these unitary and unique presentations.

Some parts of our assessment will be, though not easy, at least relatively straightforward. Those parts of a work that I called its material components and its formal features we can settle in a way that needs little discussion. Just as a human being has a material side - what Strawson calls our 'M' predicates[17] - that we can weigh, see and measure, so too we can evaluate the quality of brushwork and the angular fragmentation of pigment in painting, the pureness of tone and the maintenance of pitch in a piece of polyphony, the smoothness of surface and the fit of the joint in sculpture. Indeed there is much in our assessment of pupils' achievements in artistic work or judgments that we can measure in this way; certainly the Report of the APU on Aesthetic Development[18] properly draws attention to the amount of knowledge of content and background and of skills and techniques that have to be mastered for a pupil to be able to make a start on framing and presenting his own creative work or critical judgment within a genre. And these can be as simple or complicated as the kinds of account that have to be given of a person's 'M' predicates by such people as undertakers or medical practitioners. But both can be specified in criterial terms and both are necessary to enable operators in respect of both objects to achieve some understanding of that with which they are working.

'Necessary' but not 'sufficient'. For, as Strawson goes on to make clear, what is central to our predication of human beings as persons is in the things they do that only they and no other creatures do: 'is smiling', 'is going for a walk', 'believes in God' and 'falls in love' would be examples of our characteristic 'P-predicates. And the chief point of interest in our appreciation of the meanings of a work of art lies not in the descriptive accounts that we give of its material components or formal features but in the elucidations and formal constituents, make it uniquely what it is and what no other creature could be-its immaterial, informal, transcendent qualities of the special kind of significance and sense embodied in every living work of art.

To try to get at these, to savour them and to represent them to an audience is difficult and demanding - of time, energy, willingness to suspend disbelief and risk crossing traditional boundaries of categories, concepts and canons of logic, open-mindedness and flexibility, and of imagination. It demands a solid basis of knowledge, information and the appropriate skills and a readiness for unremitting hard work, as well as a readiness for argument and being called upon to defend one's point of view. And when we are trying to give such a defence of our judgments of the value of meaning of a work of art, we soon realise that there is no end to the things we want to mention; for these are as many layers of meaning to be stripped away in our struggle to comprehend and respond to the work as there are other artists, critics or interpreters to perceive them. Wittgenstein employs a culinary figure to exemplify this process of elucidating meanings: it is like stripping away the leaves of an artichoke.[19]

Every time we take one layer away we find another layer underneath it, ripe for our wonder and enjoyment. The only difference with works of art is that we can never come to what we can all agree is 'the heart'. And the problem is made no easier by the consideration that our own views, interpretations and responses will change over time. What we think of William Blake's perfect poem *The Sick Rose* now may be vastly different from what we made of it twenty years ago; and in twenty years' time we shall take it differently again. But it will still be perfect: it will still be a consummate fusion of truths about ourselves, others and the world.

That is perhaps one of the chief functions of those excellent products of the creative imagination that we call 'works of art': not merely to 'give delight and hurt not', not to entertain or to be a rich source of uplift for many years to come, but to give us some hitherto unknown or unexpected insight into ourselves and the human condition, to get us to see old things in a new and illuminating way. It is one of the prime characteristics of works of art that we call 'great' to provoke an arrest in the spectator and then so to work upon his/her thought and feelings as to precipitate a disclosure. And the value of such works lies in their capacity to raise our consciousness, to extend our horizons, to add vividness and the intensity of a heightened awareness to our percipience by the truths that they thus open to us. But we can only gain such access if we have the right kind of vision to perceive them and this means in turn that we must receive the right kind of training to speak and understand the languages in which these truths can be communicated. For - as one of the best-known aphorisms of Bruner has it - 'discovery, like surprise, favours the well-prepared mind'.

The principal problem with the obtaining of such understanding resides of course in the question of the intelligibility of works of art, especially when we are struggling to achieve it in relation to works that are created and presented in an essentially non-discursive mode of public communication, that nevertheless has power to move us by disclosing to us glimpses of the sublime. It is, in other words, a problem in the logic of aesthetic language, made no easier by the fact that, as it has been remarked, in aesthetics we move always from the general to the particular and not the other way. Art works are always singular and for that reason may be unamenable to elucidation in terms of general categories or concepts; indeed it seems to be a feature of the works of art and artists we call 'great' they the themselves often call into question existing forms and categories and propose new ones for our consideration, that add to the store of alternative possible ways of seeking truth in art. (It is equally likely - such is the dynamic character of the arts-that certain modes of creation and communication in them will gradually lose their power to provoke an arrest or be deemed any longer worthy of serious consideration and so become effete or fall into desuetude).

In this way the world of the arts is a paradigm of that kind of 'Open Society' which Popper sees as typifying the world of science.[20] For the kind of proposals that new works put forward, the kind of rebuttals of previous concepts and categories they suggest, are not unlike those hypotheses that scientists, historians or mathematicians put up for inspection and testing; there is a decided sense in which a novel creation in the arts function as the harbinger of a tentative theory and then invites our most strenuous efforts to falsify or amend. The problem for this kind of critical theory, however, lies again in the fact that we may often, as we consider the objects of such a review, have to be developing the appropriate sort of language for that critical appraisal as we go along - a problem not dissimilar to that of technologists who had to develop the suitable instruments and models necessary actually to build the Sydney Opera House long after the architect's design had won such acceptance and acclaim.

The problem of assessment in the arts, for this reason above all others, particularly difficult. Indeed it is difficult even to articulate, much less to understand and apply a solution. And the difficulty is exacerbated if we are working with a different set of criteria of value (supposing that we could actually articulate them) informing the aesthetic 'theory' that functions as the basis of our assessment in the arts. For it will make a considerable difference to the ways in which we defend our theories and explain our interpretations to our audience and interlocutors if we stand inside or outside the same critical or interpretive paradigm as they, be it formalist, expressive, social realist, structuralist or whatever. If we do not start to publish our work or explain it within the same basis of theoretical preconceptions there is much less than can be taken for granted and so much more that has to be elucidated and justified. That is perhaps one area in which the arts are different and more difficult than the sciences: there is so much more contentiousness and dubiety about the frameworks of meaning and intelligibility than the reasonable steady platform of public understanding and acceptance on which research and development in the sciences rests. The arts are objective all right - but it is a different sort of objectivity than that permitting and defining assertibility in the sciences and impossible to verify or vindicate by their kinds of instruments and tests. Just as it is profound misconception to ask for a demonstration of the existence of God by means of some kind of procedure having validity in the scientific realm, so it is equally fallacious to think that we can understand meaning and assess value by some model of evaluation operative in the domain of empirics and quantification in numerical terms in that realm similarly recalcitrant to that sort of 'proof'-the aesthetic.

It is, I think, particularly important to bear this is mind as and when we come to talk about the assessment of pupils' progress in acquiring the kinds of knowledge and skill that are called for in the domain of creating performing and judging appropriate to the making and evaluating of works of art. To be sure, some of the knowledge, both propositional and practical, that are appropriate to this domain can be assessed in the quantificatory mode that is also appropriate elsewhere; and Fraser Smith has a good account of the various kinds of

42

knowledge and skill that can be tested in this way [21] - the historical, sociological and cultural content and background to the lives, works, motives and maybe even the declared intentions of great artists, as well as such qualities as acuity and discrimination of perception, hand-eye co-ordination, range suppleness and extent of movement and the like. But these things that the APU document *Aesthetic Development* seems to make central features of competence in a pupil's growth in aesthetic knowledge; on the above account however they may be necessary in some sense but they are far from being sufficient. It is even doubtful whether some of this knowledge of background, for instance is even necessary to an informed aesthetic judgment; we do not, I believe, need to know anything of a Russian ballerina's personal history to be able to make a detailed evaluation of her dance. To think so is to fall into the 'intentionalist' fallacy.

Knowledge of facts and ability to exhibit certain qualities of a perceptual or locomotor sort only form part of the repertoire of the educated critic, creator or performer. The main things we look for in the products and appraisals of persons educated in the aesthetic domain subsume such knowledge and skills but also transcend them. The kinds of outcomes and attainments that we all might in general agree upon as constituting the *desiderata* that are the marks of progress in a pupil's coming to be able to produce artifacts, give performances and make judgments of an informed kind and have much less to do with an exhibition of mere technique (though that may be important as a step on the way) or a parade of relevant information, and much more to do with qualities that defy precise specification:sensitivity, delicacy, poise, balance, imaginative insight that can go off on its own, the ability to respond in the appropriate emotion, to paraphrase, to simplify and render open to inspection some of the deep levels of meaning and significance that the surface of a work conceals - above all to see or present all the many-sidedness of things in one moment or object, qualities that defy precise specification: sensitivity, delicacy, poise, balance, imaginative insight that can go off on its own. the ability to respond in the appropriate emotion, to paraphrase, to simplify and render open to inspection some of the deep levels of meaning and significance that the surface of a work conceals - above all, to see or present all the many-sidedness of things in one moment or object.

These are some, though not all, of the qualities that we may discern in the approach to a work that comes from mature and educated aesthetic development - the informed understanding and responsive appreciating that is the mark of the aesthetically educated mind, one of the happiest expressions for which is the phrase coined by Harry S. Broudy for that ability to look at and appraise works of art that stands as the valued outcome of an aesthetic education; he called it 'enlightened cherishing'.[22] The activity of such cherishing (and its activity rather than process that we think of our pupils being able to engage in) will involve bringing to bear and applying all the above qualities and others as well, of course, as knowledge of facts and skills, so as to be able to achieve some understanding of a work's many meanings in such a way that increments of illumination are added to one's own vision of reality and then maybe even to be able to clarify, explain and justify that understanding to others, so that their perspectives may be similarly transformed.[23]

When we consider these abilities of understanding, responding and explaining as desired outcomes of a pupil's aesthetic development and begin to tackle the problem of how we may best assess a pupil's progress in acquiring them - as well as establishing changes and improvements in his or her own creative or performative powers - we soon realise that we must make some exclusions in our approach to that problem. To begin with, we shall realise that the model of curriculum assessment deriving from the taxonomies of Bloom and others is not applicable; for the outcomes we are concerned to test simply do not admit of that sort of hierarchy of quantification. A splendid story is told that illustrates the ridiculousness of trying to apply such a model; it concerns the art teacher who, on being asked how he marked one of the personal qualities that he saw as being an outcome in his course - that of an increase in sensitivity-replied, 'Simple: I mark it out of 25'. Similarly, the pupil at the end of the course was asked what he had got out of the course on sensitivity; he replied, with some seriousness, 'I got a 'B'.[24]

Another exclusion will come from the realisation that a psychometric paradigm of assessment that uses a normative rather than a criterion - based approach is inappropriate. For one thing it will simply make no sense to try to draw up a curve of normal distribution for pupil's arts achievements: the nature of the activity and the uniqueness of the products are such that the outcomes at which teachers are aiming will not, again admit such an approach, quite apart from aesthetic and moral dubiousness of evaluating pupil's performance against each other and thus tacitly making the examination's basis a competitive one (a silliness that does not, unfortunately, prevent television producers making 'good television' out of programmes such as 'Young Musician of the Year'). In any case the search of the psychometric model is for qualities, abilities and achievements that have to do with a different sort of intellectual competence and skills than those we are concerned with and try to promote in the arts-with skills of analysis, dissection, partition and fragmentation: with competences of a linear, progressive and ratiocinative kind, with qualities of thinking that neuro-physiology and psychology tell us come from the left hand side of the brain. But the qualities with which we are preoccupied in an education for the development of an aesthetic insight are those associated with the right-hand hemisphere, involving intuitions, flashes of insight of a momentary but all-pervading kind, the immediate apprehension of what Polanyi called 'comprehensive wholes', the total apperception of the range of meanings in a situation or an object of contemplation and an awareness of their power to affect us-all characteristics of Ornstein's 'holistic mentation'.[25] It is the qualities of comprehensive vision and total responsiveness (a function of the 'de-differentiating' nature of works of art and maybe of religious images also) that constitute the *propria* of aesthetic understanding and that typify creative and imaginative work in those elements of the curriculum that seem particularly apt to promote their development - the expressive and performing arts. Mere intellectual attainments (important though they are) are not enough; and neither are the 'right' *attitudes* nor personal preferences (though the forming or changing of attitudes and taste are certainly also what aesthetic education is, *inter alia*, about).

For these reasons we have to search for (or, if necessary, create) and apply different modes and techniques of assessment, that are appropriate to the logic of the form of discourse in question and to the kinds of outcomes that we hold typify competence in it - to the kinds of outcomes promoted by learning and working in that community of discourse and regarded as valuable in themselves for all those who come to be able to create and communicate within it. This seems to me, at any rate, to require, as a minimum, the following:

1: that we must first work the pupils and teach them the various 'languages' in which meaning in the various worlds of arts is created and transmitted.

2: that we must then work with them at the concept of 'getting it right' in creating, communicating, understanding and valuing products and performances in them;

3: but helping them to see that meaning in the arts is plastic and plurivocal - heterogeneous both horizontally and vertically in object and *genre*, and they must be flexible, open-minded and imaginative in seeking meanings;

4: that they will have to develop that capacity for insight and responsiveness that is appropriate to the various kinds of meaning - some of them non-discursive - that are embodied in the works of art presented to them for their appreciation;

5: that pupils' perceptions of the store of possible meanings of work or awareness of their own capacity to create will be affected not only by the limits of their own powers of precision, performance, judgment and articulacy but also by the fact that products and performances in the arts have a life of their own, that grows and enlarges as time passes and experience of them grows-that, in some sense, such works are 'living beings' towards which, as Arnaud Reid insightfully points out, it is more appropriate to adopt the relationship that Buber called 'I-Thou' than the 'I-It' attitude proper to mere physical objects of an organic kind.[26]

Pupils have accordingly to learn a whole new mode of relating to works of art, that is everything other than that comprehended within the philosophy of the verification principles of the positivist paradigm(even if that were itself logically sound, which it is not). And this learning will lead quickly to the realisation that what is critically important about the development of aesthetic awareness and understanding is the increasing emphasis on a different kind of knowledge that is called for in it - that immediate awareness of and responsiveness to the fused complexities of comprehensive wholes, a mode of cognising not unlike that which Polanyi saw a special form of knowledge he called 'tacit'[27] or what others have called a kind of 'personal knowing'. In that world the canons of correctness, the criteria of significance and sense, defy precise specification in numerical or symbolic terms; the logic of that form of discourse - the peculiar concatenations of noises, marks and signs, the various materials worked in, the 'flavour' of the conventions constituting intelligibility, the considerations that make certain moves decisive - cannot be set down in the calculus or canonical notation, much less in accordance with the 'grids' or checklists to which some essays in the field of aesthetic assessment have given such pride of place. Not only do such instruments as that of the APU aesthetic development group commit the fallacy of 'composition' in proposing such 'grids' for the assessment of growth in aesthetic understanding and competence; they also make a fundamental mistake about the 'grammar' of the ways in which meaning in the arts is embodied and transmitted. So, although the work of such groups has been helpful in doing some vitally necessary 'ground-clearing' -and parts of the APU document are very good in this respect it can only serve as a preliminary stage on the way to a much more complete and satisfying account of assessment in the arts.

Two steps on that way seem to me absolutely indispensable: to begin with, arts assessors will have to go out and learn a great deal more about the techniques and forms of assessment of work in educating institutions generally than many of them already do. There is much good and valuable reading available here: the Chapter on 'Assessment' in *The Arts in Schools* contains many indications of fruitful avenues of enquiry as well as many references to sources; the work of Fraser Smith and some others in Straughan and Wrigley's *Values and Evaluation in Education* (1980) and the bibliography thereto will give workers in this field many useful suggestions for further reading and follow-up,[28] while the powerful and imaginative work of Michael Scriven on assessment generally will serve to show committed and serious-minded teachers of art subjects how very wide-ranging and various are the ways in which a great deal of a pupil's progress in their subjects can be rendered objective and measured.[29] Their reading of such works may well equip them or give them added determination to develop, or to be ready to consult and work with those who can develop, new techniques of assessment that are suitable for the arts.

Such teachers will perhaps then be able, ready and willing to embark on, or attempt to work out an approach to, what is perhaps still the greatest problem of all in the assessment of work in the arts: that of explicating the logic of the language of the arts and elucidating the criteria of what is expressible in it the problem, to repeat, of what John Dewey called the conventions of 'warranted assertability'.[30] The problem here is that the ways of meaning are complex and highly protean in character, certainly unamenable to predication in terms of formal truth-propositional functions, even when and, as we are too uncomfortably aware, that is not the case in a large number of instances meanings can be discussed and communicated in discursive terms.

But the fact that the languages of the arts are heterogeneous, complex and frequently non-discursive does not render them *in principle* beyond clarification; their grammar may be recondite, eccentric or even iconoclastic, but that does not mean that it is idiosyncratic. If that were the case works of art would be ineffable, not merely arcane; their meaning would be incapable of reception by any kind of audience but would be private fictions in their creator's head only and their secret, if he chose to keep it so, would die with him. Maybe some of the nuances of artistic meaning cannot be *said* but only *shown*;[31] but there are ways of pointing and seeing that do give us the basic building blocks for the construction of the reception and response that is self-evidently the formal intention of any artist who publishes his work. And it is these pointings and seeings that help to establish and define the limits of the artistic universe of language, into which an aesthetic education provides us with admission.

The prime problem is, then one for the philosopher and those who work in the fields of logic, language and meta-aesthetics. Work is being done and the store of understanding being added to, as any examination of recent issues of the *British Journal of Aesthetics* will show. Scruton and Sibley in this country, Nelson Goodman and Adorno in the United States are names that must rank prominently in the list of those to whom we may look for illumination in this difficult but important field. Certainly artists who seek means of clarification and teachers who need tools for application to the assessment of artists' work need not despair; the achievements of Richard Hare and George Henrik von Wright in struggling with the complexities of deontic logic to give an account of the language of morals are being emulated by those who seek to assist us in unravelling some of the complexities of the communication of ideas by means of works of art. Form, matter, content, intention, effect, consequence, structure, texture all these are features in the logic of 'talk' within and about the arts, the clarification and detailed investigation of which will give us a means of articulating those criteria that we shall need if we are to show that the arts too are objective and that work and progress in them capable of conforming to the demands of educational accountability.[32] And this task must now be undertaken by philosophers, artists and teachers of the arts; if we are to vindicate the place of the arts as a fundamental element of the curriculum of educational institutions, that the Sheffield speech of Sir Keith Joseph and the conclusions of the ILEA Hargreaves Committee have so powerfully argued they deserve.

NOTES AND REFERENCES

1. *The Arts in Schools* - principles, practice and provision. (Ed.Peter Brinson), London (Calouste Gulbenkian Foundation), 1982
2. Sir Keith Joseph speech at the North of England Education Conference on the theme 'Catastrophe or Watershed?' Sheffield, 6 January 1984, DES Press Notice 1/84.
3. *Improving Secondary Schools* - report of the Committee set up by the ILEA, under the chairmanship of Dr.D.H. Hargreaves on the Curriculum and Organisation of Secondary Schools (March 1984).
4. *Aspects of Secondary Education* - A Survey by HM Inspectors of Schools, London (HMSO), December 1979.
5. K.R. Popper, *The Logic of Scientific Discovery*, London (Hutchinson) 1974;

T.S. Kuhn, *The Structure of Scientific Revolutions*, Chicago (Chicago University Press) 1973; I. Lakatos, 'Falsification and the Methodology of Scientific Research Programmes', in I. Lakatos and A.W. Musgrave (eds.) *Criticism and the Growth of Knowledge*, Cambridge (CUP) 1870;

P. Feyerabend 'How to be a good Empiricist —' in P.H. Nidditch (ed.) *The Philosophy of Science*, London (Oxford U.P.) 1968. See also Kevin Harris Education and Knowledge, London (Routledge and Kegan Paul) 1979, ch.1.

6.   L. Wittgenstein, *Philosophical Investigations*, (Trans. G.E.M. Anscombe), Oxford (Blackwell) 1953, paras. 243, 256 and 293.
7.   G. Ryle, *The Concept of Mind*, London (Hutchinson) 1949.
8.   See D.E. Cooper, *Philosophy and the Nature of Language*, London (Longmans) 1973; ch.1; also Bernard Harrison *Introduction to the Philosophy of Language*, London (Macmillan)1979, ch.1.
9.   C.K. Ogden and I.A. Richards, *The Meaning of Meaning*, London (RKP) 1930.
10. G.H.R. Parkinson (ed.) *The Theory of Meaning*, London (OUP) 1968, 'Introduction'.
11. L. Wittgenstein, op.cit. para. 43
12. In this I follow P.F. Strawson, 'Aesthetic Appraisal and Works of Art' in his *Freedom and Resentment and Other Essays*, London (Methuen) 1974.
13. On these matters see the works of L. Wittgenstein as follows (all published in Oxford by Blackwell): 'Form of Life': *Philosophical Investigations* (1953),174,226; Blue and Brown Books (1958), 119; *Philosophical Remarks* (1975), 147; 'Language-games': Phil.Invras.7, 19-23, 130; B and B. Bks. 81; *Philosophical Grammar* (1974), 55, 140; On Certainty (1969), 559, 65.
14. L. Arnaud Reid, *Meaning in the Arts*, London (Allen and Unwin), 1969; Sonia Greger 'Aesthetic Meaning' in Proceedings of the Philosophy of Education Society of Great Britain, Vol.VI, No.2, July 1972, pp.137 ff.
15. *Heraclitus Fragment* 12 and *Plato Cratylus*, 402A in G.S. Kirk and J.E. Raven, *The Presocratic Philosophers*, Cambridge (CUP), 1957, pp.196-7.
16. A. Ehrenzweig, *The Hidden Order of Art: A Study in the Psychology of Artistic Imagination*, London (Weidenfeld and Nicholson), 1967.
17. P.F. Strawson, *Individuals-An Essay in Descriptive Metaphysics*, London (Methuen), 1958, ch.3 'Persons', pp.104-110.
18. *Aesthetic Development - a discussion document of an Exploratory Group set up the Assessment of Performance Unit*, London (DES), September 1983.
19. L. Wittgenstein, *Phil. Inv.*, para. 164; B. & B. Bks., p.125.
20. K.R. Popper, op.cit. See also his *Open Society and its Enemies*, London (RKP), 1943; and his *Objective Knowledge*, London (OUP) 1972.

21. Fraser Smith, Ch.10 'Art' in R.R. Straughan and Jack Wrigley (eds.) *Values and Evaluation*, London (Harper and Row), 1980.
22. H.S. Broudy 'Enlightened Preference and Justification', in R.A. Smith ed.) *Aesthetics and Problems of Education*, Urbana, Ill. (University of Illinois P.), 1971 See also Diane Collinson 'Aesthetic Education' in Glenn Langford and D.J. O'Connor (eds.) *New Essay in Philosophy of Education*, London (RKP), 1973.
23. On this cf D.N. Aspin 'The Arts, Education and the Community', in *Journal of Art and Design Education*, Vol.I, No.1, July 1982.
24. I am indebted to Dr Ken Robinson for this.
25. Robert J. Ornstein, *The Psychology of Consciousness*, Harmondsworth (Penguin P.), 1975.
26. L.Arnaud Reid 'Knowledge, Aesthetic Insight and Education', in *Proceedings of the Philosophy of Education Society of GB*, 1973, Vol.VIII, p.66. Also his Ways of Knowledge and Experience, London (Allen and Unwin), 1961.
27. M. Polanyi, *The Tacit Dimension*, London (RKP), 1966. See also his *Knowing and Being*, London (RKP), 1969, esp. Pt.II; and his *Personal Knowledge*, London (RKP), 1958, Pt.II, Ch. 6 sects. 4 and 12.
28. Apart from Straughan and Wrigley op.cit.sup., cf. also M. Ross (ed.) *The Aesthetic Imperative*, Oxford (Pergamon), 1981; James M. Thyne, *Principles of Examining*, London (U.L.P.), 1974; Derek M. Rowntree, *Assessing Students: How Shall We Know Them?* London (Harper and Row), 1977;
R. Montgomery, *A New Examination of Examinations*, London (RKP), 1978
M.Holt, *Evaluating the Evaluators*, London (Hodder and Stoughton), 1981 and David Satterly, *Assessment in Schools*, Oxford (Blackwell), 1981.
29. Michael Scriven, *The Methodology of Evaluation*, published by Purdue University Social Sciences - Education Consortium, USA, 1966; also R.W. Tyler, R.M. Gagne and M. Scriven, *Perspectives of Curriculum Evaluation*, Chicago (Rand McNally), 1967.
30. For an elaboration of this idea see John Dewey, Logic: *The Theory of Enquiry*, New York (Henry Holt and Co.Inc), 1938, p.134.
31. See L.Wigggenstein, *Tractatus Logico-Philosophicus*, (trans.D.F. Pears and B.F. McGuiness), London (RKP), 1961, paras. 6.42, 6.421 and, especially, 6.522: 'There are, indeed, things that cannot be put into words. They make themselves manifest. They are what is mystical'. For an elaboration of the importance of this point in the field of value generally, cf.F.A. Rizvi, *The Fact-Value Distinction and the Logic of Educational Theory*, unpublished PhD thesis, University of London, 1983, pp.45,ff.
32. See H.T. Sockett,et al., *Accountability in the English Educational System*, London (Hodder and Stoughton),1980; also Colin Lacey and Denis Lawton (eds), *Issues in Evaluation and Accountability*, London (Methuen),1981.

A TGAT PERSPECTIVE

PROFESSOR PAUL BLACK, KINGS COLLEGE, UNIVERSITY OF LONDON AND CHAIR OF TGAT (Task Group on Assessment and Testing)

The report that we produced is quite a long one: the excuse we have for that is that we did not have time to produce a short one. I really mean that, and I am in some difficulty as I do not wish to go on for two hours explaining the niceties. What I shall try to do is take a very rapid tour around it, But hope to leave time for you to ask questions about particular bits you really want to go into.

The first principle with which we started the report is that assessment is central to teaching and learning, and not marginal. It should help pupils, teachers and others to know where they are, what progress has been made, and what needs to be done next. The feedback from assessment is essential for the improvement of pupils' learning. We then go on to consider some principles upon which an assessment system can be based:

1. Criterion referencing: we should be interested in what children can, and cannot do, and not in comparing them one to another.

This is a very broad definition, and it is in terms of that broad definition that we recommend criterion referencing. I draw your attention to the fact that there is a glossary of terms at the beginning of the report that it was very necessary to provide. I know that it is a bit daunting to open a report and that is the first think that you see, but it is right that it should be.

2. Assessment should be Formative: The main purpose of assessment should be to help decide what the pupil should do next, certainly at ages 7,11 and 14. At 16 it would shift to a record of all the pupil has achieved (summative). The other purpose of assessment is Diagnostic, and the difference between that and formative assessment is that diagnostic gives you detailed information of particular strengths and weaknesses, and their caused, and helps you to plan remedial action. For a small proportion of pupils, you may need to go in detail into the reasons why they are performing extremely badly or extremely well.

That is a pretty heavy job and you would only want to do it for the minority with the particular need. The National Assessment isn't intended to do that; we recommend that extra help be made available to enable schools to make their own extra assessments for the small proportion of pupils shown to have particular problems.

3. Moderation: There should be a combination of external, and internal teachers assessments with a process of moderation to reconcile the two, and that process would be one in which teachers should take a responsible part.

4. Progression: We are talking about a National Curriculum 5-16, and thinking about assessing at several ages during that span; the criteria and the reporting should be on some single system which spans all the ages, not a system which is calibrated to make sense at one age and not in any way related to what happens at the next age. To put it another way, if a pupils is bottom of the class at age 7, they may still be bottom of the class at age 11, but we do not know from that evidence whether or not that pupil has made any progress. It may well be that they have made quite a lot of progress between the two ages, and that would be represented and reflect in a system of progression that assessed the pupil against the same set of criteria at both ages.

We spent some time in the report addressing ourselves to fears that people have about assessment, and we claim that we have attended to those fears.

There are fears that reported failure will have a bad effect and depress the pupil. That is certainly true. However a system of progression which can give pupils of all abilities targets appropriate to them so that they can know that they are making some progress, is an important factor in offsetting that concern. It would be absurd to not let pupils know if they were doing badly for fear of depressing them; the system must report to pupils and their parents where they are going.

There are fears that the relationship between teachers and parents might be put at risk. That is one we did not think we could take seriously because we feel that a more uniform system across subjects and across ages will actually help parents and help teachers in talking to them. We reflect on experience and going round the teachers in a secondary school on parents evenings and getting information from each of them on how a child is doing; usually each teacher is using a different terminology, a different scale, a different description: even I get confused, and I know a little bit about education. I don't know what the average parent can make of it. We can do better than that.

There are fears that the system will detract from the professional standing and responsibility of teachers. Well it mustn't, and if it does, it will not be any good. That is back to the 'central, not marginal' principle; we have to involve teachers, and make them responsible for working the assessment. That is to say that everything is left to their judgment entirely, which is a different issue.

Finally, there are worries about doing damage to schools through publication of results of assessment. This is probably the most difficult of the issues to resolve, and I will return to it later.

How do you set up a system of assessment?

In each foundation subject area, one ought to define the aims of education in that subject not in terms of a single piece of information, but a set of pieces of information that we call profile components. The profile represents where the pupil is in the most important areas that the subject contributes to the pupil's development. That comes from the view that 3 or 4 pieces of information are better than one. In terms of communication, and assessment is very much about communication between schools, within schools, and between the public and schools, you get better communication if you give several pieces of diverse information, but it fails if the number of pieces of information gets too large. To report a pupils progress to a parent in terms of 20 different profile components for each subject would be confusing.

We are saying to subject working groups that this is a framework within which they should work. They must tease out how many significantly different pieces of information they would like to report on as a means of communication achievement and progress in their subject. In science, there would be the concepts and knowledge, the practical and other manipulative skills of general use, and the capacity to handle open-ended investigation to solve problems using the scientific method.

The areas should be as broad as that, they encompass significantly different sets of aims, and I think that the average parent could make sense of them; each would have its own assessment methods. It is very important in your (the arts) subject areas to talk around this idea and work out which areas would form appropriate profile components.

What are tests?

We are working against the public perception that tests are only a narrow fixed response things taken with fear and trembling at set times. We tried to give examples of test items to show the variety of types of question, some involve writing, some discussion, some involve performing (taking a measurements or making something). There can be quite systematic appraisal of what is being done by procedures and rules in which teachers can be trained. The term 'test' can be substituted by the phrase 'assessment task' to signify this broader approach - without in any way implying that procedures should be less rigorous or results less reliable.

Why should people have confidence in the system and its results? If the results fairly reflect the pupil's ability, then people will have confidence in the test. When being assessed, pupils often fail to do justice to themselves, but rarely show up better than their actual ability. In order to overcome this, you should use a variety of methods and look very carefully at any discrepancies between the various outcomes.

Teachers internal assessments done in the 'natural' context, and with tasks that make sense to the pupils and are part of their normal learning, have very great strength. These cannot be replaced entirely by external, artificial, tests completed in a short time. There is plenty of evidence however, that teachers find it difficult to relate their own expectations of performance at any level with that of other teachers in the same or other schools. There is also evidence from some assessment projects in the lower part of secondary schools, that when teachers from different schools get together to systematically assess what their pupils are doing, they find it extremely difficult to establish the simple minimum that every pupil gets out of each teacher's teaching. Teachers who had never looked at assessment collectively and sharply the way they were doing there, found that the actual performance of the lower half of classes came as a surprise:

they performed much less well than expected by the teachers. So internal assessment alone will not give confidence.

You need a combination of both internal and external assessment procedures; we have recommended that this de dome by group-moderation. That is to say, groups of teachers should get together and they should administer national assessment tasks with their pupils according to set rules, and they should set them on the same scales as their own assessment and then compare the distributions of the two. We are very keen that the comparison should be on distributions; that is to say, if you have, say, three levels at the age of 7, what you should be looking at is that in a group of pupils, 10% are at level one, 80% level two, and 10% level three. That is very different from 20%, 60%, 20%. These two distributions have the same average, but are very different distributions. These two distributions have the same average, but are very different distributions. Press reports that we are intending to publish averages are incorrect. It is the distributions that should be adjusted in group moderation.

We are keen that assessments at 7, 11, 14 and 16 should be carried out by teachers who have known the pupils for some time, and not by teachers in the schools to which pupils have just moved. For example, good assessment, with some confidence in the standards and using criteria that are common between schools, at age 11 would be an important asset in the transition to secondary schools by providing better information between the feeder schools and the secondary schools.

If you want to represent progression, then you must have a common scale of performance across ages. We recommend that this scale be expressed as a set of levels 1 to 10. The levels should be defined in very broad terms as having a spacing which is the average change in pupils performance over a couple of years, so that the median pupil between 7 and 16 years will go over about four and a half such levels. There is evidence that the spread of pupils is much larger than that so that you would need at 10 levels to cover the full range of ability. So what we are proposing is that in each profile component you have a set of 10 levels where at age 7 the median pupil is at level 2, at age 11 the median pupil is at level 4, and at age 14 the median pupil is at level 5 or 6 and at 16 the median pupil is at level 7 or 8. That would set up a system with a uniform change of one level every two years. That uniform, linear slope is not created by some psychometric magic, we haven't somehow discovered that children's learning is linear. It is made linear: to fix the levels to start with, you take the median pupil to fix the criteria for each level in terms of what you know. After that we should work in terms of the criteria, and the levels are then criterion referenced.

We have also indicated the expected distribution of performance at any one age. That is highly speculative; we also put something there about where GCSE grading corresponds at age 16; that is speculative too. These features are to be discovered, and may differ from one profile component to another, and from one subject to another. But one of the things that we are trying to emphasise is that we have a single system, and we really have to think of this not as testing everyone by a test mode for one particular age and - say - holding them back by this system: 'why can't they take the test earlier?' for example. That is not the proposition. The proposition is that you may have to provide children with differentiated tests, particularly the older ages, and you find out where their progress has taken them on the overall (cross-age) scale at a particular time. You don't inhibit their progress through the work you do with them, you simply provide the assessment appropriate to where they are.

So the system is an overlay at particular ages on what teachers are doing already and will be doing at all ages. The difficulty about the system is not mainly an assessment difficulty, but it is the curriculum implication of linking improved ideas about progression expressed in the attainment targets of the national curriculum with formative assessment to guide pupils learning accordingly. When the spreads of attainment begin to be more sharply realised, I believe it will create a lot more difficulty about how to treat the variety of abilities and rates of progression that children actually show. I don't think that we have faced those difficulties sufficiently well so far.

Looking at the primary level at age 7, if you have three or four profile components in each of 9, 10 or 11 foundation subjects, then the class teacher of 7 year olds will have to generate evidence about where the pupils are on the levels in about forty different profile components. That is clearly impossible. It actually reflects some of the difficulties with the way in which the National Curriculum has been specified in terms of subjects right across the whole age range. This throws up problems with the younger ages, and what we have said is that at age 7, we must have a smaller number of profile components; those which are in some sense basic, the ones you should be emphasising with young children. There should be a small number that you can usefully handle in order to derive information about the really important components needed at that stage for detecting particular excellence or particular difficulty. At older ages, you can expand the components in a related way that is evolutionary and makes a coherent pattern. In secondary school, you have subjects in boxes, each with about four profile components, but in primary, you won't have subject boxes, but the profile components will be more general and basic. For later ages these will split and elaborate, either to form the full elaboration of a subject, or to split between subjects, for instance, measurement and observation may be a single unitary theme at age seven and split between mathematics and science later on.

We will look at age 11 as being an intermediate phase involving proto-subjects giving that information which is useful for preparation for work in the subjects at secondary stage. The general idea of an evolutionary and organic relationship between profile components at different ages will have to be worked by collaboration between the subject working groups.

Another aspect that follows from that is that it will be very important for each subject group to think pretty hard about profile components which should overlap. Some should be identical between different subjects, and that should be negotiated. Others could be similar in their specification, if one argues that they are context bound to this subject or that subject: nevertheless, there should be some similarity between them so you can compare pupils performance on that profile component between the particular subjects. The negotiation required becomes easier and more consistent when the separate profile components are seen as evolving from common ones at earlier ages. I am conscious that is a gleam in the eye, and it will take an enormous amount of work to sort it out in practice. But that it should be sorted out is extremely important because that is the way in which cross-curricular values and issues can be given due attention in the national curriculum. I should say that we have not found that the Department or Ministers have any difficulty with this proposition and that so far they have expressed general agreement with it.

Also, the subject working groups are working quite hard on the commonality of profile components. We have also recommended that there should be a single group to unify and coordinate the work at primary level.

Subject working groups working independently at primary level couldn't do the job. There has recently been established a primary sub-group which serves the science and maths working groups and my task group and will incorporate people from the other working groups as they are established. That group has the responsibility for looking after this coordination and having a dialogue with the subject working groups for this purpose.

The difficulty with all of this is that we all need far more time, and it would have been much easier if the *Task Group on Assessment* and most of seven subject working groups had been working in parallel. The exigencies of time mean that it is not possible for the different subject working groups to have dialogue in this way. The Science group will have finished when the English group has been in existence for only a short time, and before the History or Geography groups have every been set up. Because they are staggered, the coordination needed will be very hard to set up. it will be much easier when the new National Curriculum Council is set up, for then there will be an agency that can take on the coordination work.

I shall cover one more, very sensitive, issue, and that is reporting and publication. It has attracted more attention than any other. We have said that reporting is different from publication; reporting is for people who need to know, (pupils, parents, governors and so on). Age 7 results have to be *reported*. Publication is opening it out for everybody, and age 7 results should *not* be published. Our recommendation were as follows:

We recommend that national assessment results for pupils at age 11, aggregated at school level, should be published as part of each primary school's report. We recommend that there should be no requirement to publish results for pupils at age 7.

We recommend that national assessment results for pupils at age 14 and 16, aggregated at school level should be published as part of each school's report.

We have suggested that, for example, secondary schools could put into such a report if they wish, the attainments of their pupils on entry so that the value they have added can be appraised. We are not in favour of this being done by a set formula as a requirement.

We know well that socioeconomic background is the biggest single determinate of what schools can do. If you don't take account of that, you will misjudge a school and parents might be misled in choosing the best school for their child. We have said that those socioeconomic factors should be talked about, discussed, and data given about them in school reports, and that local authorities should help in doing that. We have not recommended the publication results adjusted statistically for socioeconomic backgrounds: it is extremely difficult to explain statistically adjusted results to parents. They have been doing this is the State of California for some time and have just given it up because parents couldn't make sense of it.

We have stressed that there should be a five-year period of phasing in, and that pupils aged 7 should only be assessed on holistic tasks, not on set formal tests. Teachers should use some small project which has been designed, and trialled externally, in which pupils can get interest and involved, and whilst they are doing it, evidence about their abilities to write something, to discuss, to produce a diagram or a poster about, to construct something in a simple way, should be evoked and recorded. In that way the profile components can be extracted from pupils' action and work in particular tasks, and that should be the only procedure for assessments at age 7. The shift into more formal assessment should happen later.

Things like that have been done, they are being used, and are rather like what is going on in many primary schools now. But the difference is that teachers at primary level will have to look far more sharply at quite what they are trying to achieve with such work than they have done in the past, and indeed that would be an advantage.

PAPERS FROM THE CHAIR FOR THE NAEA CONFERENCE, October, 1988

During the two days of October 25th and 26th, 1988, the National Association for Education in the Arts held a specially arranged conference in London at North Westminster school to tackle the issue of assessment in the arts in the context of the National Curriculum. The agreed format of the event was that on the first day invited small groups representing the various arts would try to identify the way forward, working from a paper circulated in advance by the Chairman. They then would engage in open discussion with the membership on the second day which around 100 people attended. A stimulating and committed debate ensued. It became very clear that members of NAEA who attended this event were convinced that assessment in the arts is inevitable, desirable and feasible. There are, of course, difficulties and dangers and the issues cannot be fudged. Much work remains to be done but the conference demonstrated that arts educators are on the move.

It needs to be said that the spirit of the conference was highly constructive and the intellectual level of discussion was often very high, conducted as it was with great concern and energy. The outcome is not easily documented and regretfully, it is not possible to here reproduce the views of the working groups and individuals. These appear in *Take-Up* No. 8. It was clear that arts educators are thinking hard and sensitively about what they do and are very positive on the issue of assessment. They want to get it right.

INTRODUCTION: THE FEASIBILITY OF ASSESSMENT IN THE ARTS

PROFESSOR KEITH SWANWICK, INSTITUTE OF EDUCATION, UNIVERSITY OF LONDON

The National Association for Education in the Arts has taken a lively interest in the policies and legislation that move our schools towards a National Curriculum and has been especially active on the issue of assessment. At our conference in October 1987, we were joined by the Minister of State, Angela Rumbold, the Labour MP, Derek Fatchett and David Hargreaves, then Chief Inspector for ILEA. We had at that time already identified some of the crucial arguments that arts educators might wish to make. It seems important to rehearse these again here, for they do recur whenever the spectre of assessment haunts the educational scene.

One major worry is the promulgation of a simplistic acceptance of an objectives model of the curriculum. As I said on the 28th of October 1987 (*Take-Up* 6):

> Phrases like 'setting clear objectives' and having realistic 'expectations' along with the idea of 'attainment targets', communicate the sense of a curriculum 'out there', something precise and objective, as real as the milk bottle on the doorstep. Indeed, the curious phrase inherited from Sir Keith Joseph, 'the delivery of the curriculum', carries with it just that image of the milk float with its neatly stacked bottles and cartons; the product measured out precisely; labelled blue or gold top; sterilised yet nourishing, delivered. Let us be clear what this means for classroom transactions in general: teachers are to know in advance what learning outcomes are to be brought about; they are to devise activities to ensure that pupils achieve them; they are to have ways of assessing the level of this achievement. Objectives are to do with prediction, knowing in advance where we are going.

The theoretical template at work here is that of industrial production, conceiving of education as the manufacture of pre-specified objects. We know that working as if on a conveyor belt is hardly likely to equip pupils 'for the challenges of employment in tomorrow's world', a world where independence of thought and the ability to see new possibilities may be much more important than merely meeting other people's objectives and quotas.

We are told in The National Curriculum 5-16 that having 'attainment targets' is 'a proven and essential way towards raising standards of achievement'. These targets will be the standards used for assessment and 'at the heart of the assessment process there will be nationally prescribed tests' which will supplement individual teachers' assessments. Clearly, testing is thought to be essential, both in the interests of quality control, which is important for the consumer (the nation generally and parents in particular?), and as a spur to the labour force (teachers and students?). The metaphor of industrial accountancy is at work here. Again, I countered this view in 1987.

We know what is likely to happen here in the real world of school. Teachers will teach towards the tests, especially under conditions of appraisal. But are tests always the best method of assessment? Would a test be a realistic technique for assessing E.M. Forster's ability as a novelist, Rembrandt as a painter or Ravi Shankir as a musician or Rutherford as a scientist? Are tests always suitable for assessing childrens' ability to write cogently, to speak convincingly, to design, draw, paint, sing, play and dance?

These questions are raised once again here because it might appear to some arts educators that my own position is to the right of centre on this issue. I do not accept that the assumptions behind the simplistic and unrealistic view that testing as a device can usually tell us what is worth knowing. Nor do I believe that any National Curriculum can cover all but a fraction of worthwhile knowledge and experience or that schools are the only agents of learning, let alone that testing will motivate students and teachers to work and engage with what is valuable in our culture. But this does not absolve us from a good deal of hard thinking and careful and systematic observation of what children actually do and can do in the arts. Again, let me quote from the *Take-Up* No. 6.

> We need to work together towards more sensitive and helpful assessment of children's work, generating a decent theory which describes, explains and starts to predict artistic development, though never the outcome of any particular art project - that would violate the enterprise. This is necessary, not because it has is required by our other people but because it is essential for the quality of our own work as teachers. Testing as such will never be of much if any value to us. We ought though, to be able to sustain an alternative vision of assessment as criticism, criticism of the folio, the poem, the dance, the improvisation, the performance, the composition, the design, the artifact - objects and events from the real world.

Fortunately, Professor Paul Black and his *Task Group on Assessment and Testing* have made it quite obvious that the crude version of assessment as simply standardised testing should be replaced by the more liberal and educationally more profitable idea of standard assessment tasks, a concept greatly advantageous to arts educators. I would also emphasise the earlier point: there is often confusion here. It might well be possible to identify crucial elements of artistic experience and even the most likely sequence of artistic development, but this is not to assume that the outcome of a child's artistic work can be known in advance.

Given a particular curriculum activity, some learning is fairly predictable and can therefore be planned in a fairly sequential way, putting down markers for achievement and identifying the stages that most pupils might follow in order to achieve. But we also have to be sensitive to alternative learning outcomes, those valued steps forward which can never be predicated by national committees or even the teacher on the spot, but which make all the difference to the development of each individual. Standardised production has no place in any model of arts education. They are concerned with what is new and fresh, with what is unique. We too are looking for 'excellence'; excellence of a rather different kind from the achievement of basic functional competences, excellence which can be recognised by the sensitive observer and may be drawn out by well-conceived curriculum tasks.

Before embarking on the substance and outcomes of the NAEA Symposium in October 1988, I should like to clear up one other difficulty. This concerns the relationship between assessment of pupils as individuals and the evaluation of schools as living communities. A school is a social organism, not a teaching machine. As I said in my earlier paper:

> The quality of the life of this organism depends on many things; but colour and line, gesture and movement, dance and song, ceremony and ritual, are among the elements that sustain the life of human societies and, while tending towards a communal sense, perhaps even a feeling of 'oneness', also throw us back on ourselves, causing us to reappraise ourselves, our relationships and the values of the community in which we find ourselves.

> The arts are an essential part of the fabric of living. No cohesive community exists without recourse to the range of symbolic discourse we call the arts. They must also be part of the fabric of schools, if schools are to be places where motivation is present, where great traditions are respected and entered into, where human values are celebrated.

Having said all of this, and it needs to be said, we are still faced by the challenge of pupil assessment. In *Take-Up* 7, Gillian Robinson warns us against assessment; fearing that technical skill will be all that matters, that attempts will be made to judge creativity, that the personal tastes of assessors will intrude, that the experience of being labelled a 'failure' will 'spell disaster for the future response of the child'. Crucially for her and for many others, the heart of the matter lies in the statement by Louis Arnaud Reid, that 'responsiveness cannot adequately be tested'. But then, can responsiveness be observed at all? It is hardly sufficient to provide 'relevant activities' and leave it at that. Teachers themselves have do develop the capacity, the understanding to respond to the work. Nor is it enough to advocate assessing 'engagement in the activity rather than the product'. Even if we regard the process of engagement as crucial, as indeed it is, we are still confronted with the products themselves; what a child actually says, does or makes, what is produced.

To ignore such vital evidence - evidence which is capable of illuminating the processes - is surely not being advocated. We are still left with our responsibilities as sensitive critics to try to make sense of what has been produced and respond appropriately as teachers. For it would be to underestimate children to assume that what they make, say, or do is not part of a continuum of artistic work, interleaved with a variety of influences traditions, conventions and the work of those adults who may actually be paid to function as musicians, actors, writers, dancers, visual artists or designers. The same fundamental criteria by which we try to interpret works or art and art events for ourselves are surely integral to assessment in school. Children are not a sub-species of humanity producing 'sub' art. What they produce demands attention and respect and they have a right to expect their teachers to understand something of what it is that makes things 'work' or not. They expect thoughtful, insightful and sensitive criticism, in the best sense of that word. It is for this reason that the members of NAEA at the October Conference, 1988 were sent in advance the following paper. The model there put forward as a starting point is the result of several years careful research specifically into the musical compositions of children and into the literature on creativity and artistic development. It can be viewed in several ways.

Firstly, it identifies the vital elements of musical experience, and I think from the available evidence, of artistic experience more widely. When a person engages in an art there seem to be four major related, though different sets of qualities. We relate to the surface of sensory materials, perhaps delighting in them, coming to discriminate between them and maybe learning to master them in a skilful way; we become aware of expressive character - not our personal reaction but the identification of mood, atmosphere, gesture and the more specific character of a role or visual image; we see these gestures together in a coherent form; and we may come to a sustained value commitment to the significance of these encounters, perhaps eager to find out more about them and their social and human contexts.

Whatever we choose to call them; Materials, Expression, Form and Value are the most commonly identified elements in artistic experience and it must be from these that any assessment profile be constructed.

Secondly, the model can be seen as developmental, arising as it does from a study of the work of children over the years of schooling and even before. To that extent it is indeed linear, that is to say it can be used to describe the differences that seem most commonly to emerge as children grow and develop and as they respond to the stimulation of the environment, including schools. Presumably there is nothing wrong with this assumption; it seems to work quite well in other areas; thus, we do not generally expect a child of 5 to be able to drive on the public highway, a child of 8 to design an engine or someone of 10 to write a commercially successful play. Of course there are exceptions but we need have no fear of overlooking prodigies or of not noticing the exceptional. It is precisely because we have some sense of what is normally expected that we can spot the unusual so easily. So let us not get too alarmed by a proposal which appears to try to uncover the most usual sequence of artistic development. A reasonably accurate map here would be most helpful to teachers.

Thirdly, the model can be seen as truly spiral, re-entered at every artistic encounter. As a classroom or studio dynamic it would then serve to remind us of what is involved when we begin to explore certain materials; of the shifts towards expression, form and value that necessarily are part of the transaction, sustaining the engagement.

Bearing these antecedents in mind, the following paper can perhaps be seen in a broader context, though the specific major task was to respond the challenge of finding profile components for each art. At least we have begun that work. The paper is presented here as it was to the conference, though with hindsight it could have been somewhat different. In the lively following professional discourse, it turned out that there were other models in the process of development and these surfaced as the conference proceeded. We were certainly not starting from zero. During the discussion and in subsequent papers from working groups and individuals, there emerged a range of attitudes to and possibilities for assessment in the arts. Though there appeared to be some divergence of views it became apparent that assessment was considered to be both inevitable *and* desirable. The central problems concern the appropriateness of particular forms of assessment and the use of alternative terminologies which tended to hide broad conceptual agreement.

BRIEFING PAPER FROM THE CHAIRMAN: ON ASSESSMENT

The Need

The association has agreed to urgently consider ways of responding to the issue of assessment within the National Curriculum. Whether the Arts are only to have Guidelines or be more rigorously assessed, there is still a recognised need to articulate a sense of progression within Arts curricula and it would seem in keeping with the rest of the scheme to work to the ages of 7, 11, 14 and 16, even if these seem somewhat arbitrary.

NAEA is well constituted to form a task group on assessment in the Arts. Over several years, its conferences and publications have been public demonstrations of its concern, and witness to the range of experience of its members and its professional standing. Recent conferences have included among the speakers Angela Rumbold, the Minister of State for Education and the Chairman of TGAT, Professor Paul Black. At the end of the conference on Assessment in the Arts, 3 March, 1988, it was agreed to set up a one-off symposium in an attempt to be more specific about the kind of learning outcomes that might be anticipated as a consequence of the provision of the Arts in schools. Two days spent in a well-organised way would seem potentially profitable and may help to place the Arts in a stronger position against the time the subject groups are established. What follows is a briefing paper for this assignment for conference participants to read beforehand.

The Challenge

The Task Group on Assessment and Testing (TGAT, 1988) has recommended identifying profile components, 'a cluster of attainment targets which have some homogeneity in relation to the skills, knowledge and understanding which the subject promotes'. Whether there are to be separate groups for Music and Art or a single arts group, at some stage there will be a necessity for work on specific arts activities. Any statements about components must therefore include those elements unique to any single art as well as those which the arts may share between them and possibly also with other areas of the curriculum.

We recommend that an individual subject should report a small number (preferably no more than four and never more than six) profile components. (35)

The model to be utilised is crucial and must be negotiated and mutually understood before any productive discussion can take place on detail. I would suggest that the earlier APU model is nearly but not quite serviceable for our purposes of identifying profile components (1983). The four components there proposed need organising into a dynamic structure, backed by research into how children develop in the arts.

They are:

Knowledge of Contexts (historical, social, technical terminology)

Facilitating Skills (manipulative, discriminatory, notational)
Artistic Appraisals (of expressive and structural elements)
Personal Values (attitudes)
These are not so remote from the more generally invoked cross-curriculum concepts of knowledge (ordered information), skill, (control of material) understanding ('The ability to select and use knowledge and skills over a variety of contexts to meet a variety of demands', Black) and attitudes (value positions). Understanding and Artistic Appraisals have more than a superficial relationship. Artistic Appraisals are thought of as the apprehension of 'the particular object or event before us', whether made or in the making; that is to say, the ability to bring knowledge and skills to an artistic focus.

A Model Based On Research

Elsewhere, I have proposed a model for music based on a study of childrens's compositions (Swanwick and Tillman, 1986 and Swanwick 1988). There is also corroborative work by others in music and across the arts, including that of the APU (Ross, 1984, Gardner, 1983). Basically, the elements of this model form dynamic pairs, each pair grouped around a concept not unlike those of the APU Report (1983), though expressive and structural elements have been separated out from each other - they are very different components of artistic experience. (Knowledge of Contexts is left on one side, since this seems best assessed by its presence in artistic work and workshop talk as it takes place across the model.)

These pairings are best read from the bottom up, the most likely developmental sequence. The left-hand side represents the response and contribution of individuals engaged in an arts activity: the right-hand side takes in the idea of social sharing. The model is best pictured as a spiral, though in this case with specific reference to music.

MUSICAL DEVELOPMENT

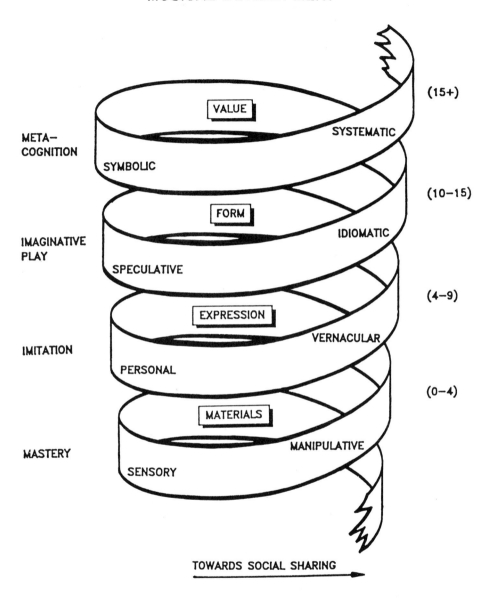

Swanwick and Tillman — 1985

The secret of assessment seems to be to take the right hand side of the spiral, the 'public' or social side, and find criterion descriptions for manipulative, vernacular and idiomatic. By definition, the manipulative mode is to do with fundamental control of sensory materials, while the vernacular is about the further exploitation of materials within the more demanding context of broadly recognisable conventions, the commonplaces of artistic production: idiomatic achievement requires awareness and fluency within consistent styles.

There are then, (at least) three qualitatively different levels of artistic control which could be summarised thus:

minimal materials (manipulative) centring on the ability to control and discriminate at a non-sequential level; perhaps simply repeating sounds, or making and identifying single gestures, movements, brush strokes and other forming actions;

limited materials (vernacular) signifies the ability to produce and identify conventional patterns; musical phrases, design motifs, sequences of movement, routines of dance or dramatic gesture; technically developed materials (idiomatic) indicates that recognisable stylistic devices have been assimilated into a repertory of artistic action and perception. Thus we can see that there might be a hierarchy of artistic ordering, from relatively simple and single acts to the organisation of combined elements into a recognisable and cohesive style. From these points of critical judgment it is then possible to begin to qualify the descriptions with reference to the related elements on the left-hand side of the spiral.

The levels of the grades given here suggested are negotiable, as are the details of the descriptions; but the dynamic structure appears to have validity and from this model we could find 8 levels in part response to the proposal in the TGAT paper that 10 levels should be specified for each profile component. Each statement is a fusion of the four profile components.

Possible criterion descriptions

Level 1: SENSORY Intermittent control of minimal materials is associated with little or no expressive characterisation. There are no identifiable structural relationships and the evolution of the work may depend heavily on technical accidents which are not exploited.

Level 2: MANIPULATIVE Minimal materials are carefully and consistently negotiated with little expressive characterisation. Structural ordering may be arbitrary, rambling or repetitious and will lack cohesion and internal logic.

Level 3: PERSONAL EXPRESSIVENESS The mastery of limited materials, though not always total, is sufficient to make artistic characterisation possible. There is clearly identifiable mood, atmosphere characterisation or gesture, though loosely organised in a fairly spontaneous manner.

Level 4: VERNACULAR Limited materials are managed consistently. The vocabulary of expression lies within recognisable conventions. There may be much repetition but will be little contrast, transformation or development and the work will be fairly predictable.

Level 5: SPECULATIVE Limited materials are generally well handled and though expressive characterisation may be fairly conventional, it will be structured in interesting, possibly experimental ways. There may be variation, transformation and contrast of ideas and the work will hold the attention, possibly eliciting surprises.

Level 6: IDIOMATIC Technically developed materials embody expressive and structural elements organised within a coherent style. There will be imaginative structural juxtapositions taking place over a time period long enough to demonstrate an ability to sustain and develop artistic thought.

Level 7: SYMBOLIC Technical mastery serves artistic communication. The spectator or listener's attention is focussed on formal relationships and expressive character which are fused together in an impressive, coherent and original statement, made with commitment.

Level 8: SYSTEMATIC There will be evidence of a high level of artistic organisation. Work may be based on new systems and organising principles, possibly using new technologies to systematically generate an original artistic language.

TGAT suggested the following distribution of levels by age, a suggestion which I have followed here. I am, therefore, suggesting four profile components, each with the possibility of inflexion up or down: Materials; Expression; Form; Value.

7 years	levels 1,2,3
11 years	levels 3,4,5
14 years	levels 4,5,6,7
16 years	levels 4,5,6,7,8

I ought to stress that these approximations to the TGAT proposals are provisional and open to change, as are the criteria descriptions. The overall model, however, seems to have some durability. There are also problems with the assessment of value attitudes, though I believe we should try to tackle these, since the experience of value seems crucial to arts encounters.

Standard Assessment Tasks

The concept of 'standard assessment tasks' is TGAT'S answer to the demand for standardisation. This represents a subtle shift from standardised *tests* and is much more liberal in the view it takes of the curriculum and of assessment.

We recommend that the national system should employ tests for which a wide range of modes of presentation, operation and response should be used so that each may be valid in relation to the attainment targets assessed. These particular tests should be called 'standard assessment tasks' and they should be so designed that flexibility of form and use is allowed wherever this can be consistent with national comparability of results. (50)

This is very important for us. We could envisage a number of tasks in the arts which would function as tests in this broad usage of the term, not confined to paper and pencil exercises or multiple choice questions. Art objects and events themselves would be our 'tests', perhaps based on limited small-scale projects. The trick would be to see that the 'tasks' were indeed standardised - that is to say, commonly set - and to ensure that these were assessed in as consistent a way as is possible.

Action

It is assumed that we are not fundamentally set against the idea of assessment. This issue will not be debated at this conference. It is further assumed that we are not opposed to making our criteria public, putting our cards on the table, although we acknowledge that formal assessment has limitations and that important transactions may be overlooked.

We might try to test out the model in the following way.

The four proposed profile components would be:

MATERIALS — EXPRESSION — FORM — VALUE

Judgments in these areas are first made in the public domains of the manipulative, vernacular, idiomatic and systematic. These can be further inflected or coloured by the degree to which the sensory, personal, speculative and symbolic appear to be present. This gives 8 levels. If we wish to approximate more closely to the TGAT proposal of 10 levels, through from age 7 to 16, then we could add an element at the bottom, where there is no evidence at all of sensory stirring (I would hope pretty rare) and a further element at the top, where the systematic valuing of arts activities produces an unusually substantial body of work. However, I think it hardly necessary to get into this - yet.

I suggest that we evaluate, refine and develop the criterion statements given above:

a) for each art

b) against the age ranges indicated by TGAT

And that we:

c) try to agree the outline of a positive statement of the position of NAEA on assessment in the Arts which would include indications of the 'standardised tasks' proposed by TGAT. I take it that these might be organised under the APU headings of Forming; Performing; Audience/Critic?

REFERENCES

DES (1983) Assessment of Performance Unit: *Aesthetic Development.*
DES (1988 *A Report* from the National Curriculum Task Group on Assessment and Testing.
Gardner, H. (1983) *Frames of Mind*, London: Paladin Books, 1985.
Ross, M. (1984) *The Aesthetic Impulse*, Oxford: Pergamon Press.
Swanwick, K. and Tillman, J. (1986) The Sequence of Musical Development, *British Journal of Music Education*, Cambridge University Press, Vol. 3, No. 3.
Swanwick, K. (1988) *Music, Mind and Education*, London: Routledge.

PART THREE

THE ARTS BEYOND THE CURRICULUM

The focus of these papers is to place the arts in relation to the wider world beyond schools. Each contributor has a distinctive 'voice', Peter Abbs being particularly concerned to urge arts educators to look for a common aesthetic, giving back a place to the idea of a received culture which can be creatively interpreted by individuals. John Blacking offers us a challenging view of the arts within a shrinking world, where cultural borrowing is inevitable and where stereotyping by art-work should be as unthinkable as any other form of crude labelling process.

THE ARTS, AESTHETIC EDUCATION AND THE PUBLIC REALM

PETER ABBS, UNIVERSITY OF SUSSEX

'Few are daring enough to connect the time assigned to one human life with the time of all humanity'. Milosz

In January 1961 in an essay entitled *Against Dryness, a Polemical Sketch*, Iris Murdoch wrote:

> We no longer see man against a background of values, of realities, which transcend him. We picture man as a brave naked will surrounded by an easily comprehended empirical world. For the hard idea of truth we have substituted a facile idea of sincerity. What we have never had, of course, is a satisfactory Liberal theory of personality, a theory of man as free and separate and related to a rich and complicated world from which, as a moral being, he has much to learn. We have bought the Liberal theory as it stands, because we have wished to encourage people to think of themselves as free, at the cost of surrendering the background.[1]

I think these observations neglected then, can now be seen, nearly 30 years later, to have a prophetic quality. During the 60's and 70's across the teaching of the arts there was a marked tendency 'to surrender the background', to disown any constraining idea of transpersonal truth or any conception of the symbolic realm broader than the immediate, the so called 'relevant' and contemporary. The actual word 'background' may be too static to convey the vast interacting field of any symbolic discipline or the vital power of received cultures which are (even when denied) always active and reactive in our lives; but let the word 'background' remain for it is clearly intended to refer to something larger than the isolated self, 'a rich and complicated' world against which the immediate actions in the foreground can be read and at least partially understood. In the same sketch Iris Murdoch claimed that 'the individual is pictured as solitary and free. There is no transcendent reality, there are no degrees of freedom' and against what she saw as the disintegrating subjectivity of individual life, with its sole criterion of sincerity, she called for ' a new vocabulary of attention', ethical, cultural and transcendent.

What many are now arguing for in arts education has a direct relationship with Iris Murdoch's claims. There is a desire to restore the notions of 'truth' and 'background' or what might be better named 'the need for transpersonal meaning' and 'the value of the symbolic field'. And this, in turn, reflects deep preoccupations in our society at large. It is, for example, highly significant that the art which is now most constantly discussed in the media is architecture, the most public, the most social, the most 'objective' of all art-forms. Prince Charles' recent call for a common code of good practice to limit private whims and market barbarism, to establish a civic aesthetic, such as was used in the construction of the beautiful Italian Renaissance towns, is symptomatic. Whether in these vociferous and fierce debates one is more sympathetic to Price Charles or to Richard Rogers is, in this context, secondary. What is most manifest is that the debates are over rival version of the good society, of the public realm, of our collective future, both nationally, internationally, and ecologically. The deep concerns are markedly different from those that structured the dominant debates in the 60's and 70's and, historically, have to be understood as a profound reaction against them.

In this lecture I want to defend this commitment to the transpersonal symbolic order and to reflect on those two vast intellectual movements of the European mind which, dialectically, have given birth to it: Modernism and Progressivism. This is a monumental theme, but in this paper I wan to reexamine the argument through a single focus, the work of Herbert Read in whose many volumes the two movements often come together to exert a profound - and often very positive - influence on both cultural life and educational practice. But now it is essential to consider some of the inadequate and negative elements in the argument. First, I will consider the partial and disfiguring elements in Read's aesthetic for education and then go on to consider his own critical responses to much of Modernism in the later years of his life.

One of the central protagonists in the story of Modernism and Progressivism in Britain must be Herbert Read who was so influential both in the art-world and in the educational world. Read played a major part in establishing the Institute of Contemporary Art (1947), then the Society for Education through Art and the International Society for Education through Art (under UNESCO in 1951). For many reasons Read's influence, bringing Modernism and Progressivism together, has now become deeply questionable. In a lecture given at Liverpool University in February 1981, considering the educational influence of Herbert Read, Ernst Gombrich has this to say:

> When I once lectured to a teachers' training class I was firmly told in the discussion that no teacher must ever show what he personally likes since he must not influence the child. I was even told elsewhere that visits to art museums by schoolchildren were frowned upon by teachers, who alleged that the late Sir Herbert Read put freshness and originality above every other concern. But why allow one self to be influenced by Herbert Read and not by Rembrandt? Why teach the child the words of our language but not the images of our tradition?[2]

Gombrich's target was, in no way, arbitrary. For years Herbert Read's *Education Through Art* - his most successful book (in 1943 the first printing of 2,000 copies was sold almost immediately) - had been the only seminal book on art education and for decades Read had expounded on the necessary principle of modernity, a principle which became in his writings more and more eclectic and elastic. In the 1930's his position had, however, been openly revolutionary. In 1933 in *Art Now* Read had declared 'the aim of five centuries of European effort is openly

74

abandoned' and then in 1935 is claimed: 'everywhere the greatest obstacle to the new social reality is the existence of the cultural heritage of the past'. In the same address Read applauded Walter Gropius' conception of a new architecture based not on memory but on a pure factional geometry. Later, as I will show, Herbert Read was to express considerable disillusionment with the artistic achievement of Modernism but before examining the nature of that unease, expressed in a number of essays and particularly in the last lecture he gave in 1968, I want to examine Read's conception of a progressive arts education.

At the outset it is important to notice that there is a certain affinity between the concepts of Modernism and Progressivism; both words bear within them an orientation to time a positive forward-looking disposition. The word Modernism derives from the word modo meaning 'just now'. In the lexicon of Modernism this orientation of time is invariably celebrated and dramatised. It can be seen in the concept of the 'avant-garde' (deriving from the French for the Vanguard, the military spear-head at the front of the assault) and in the name of, for example, a movement like Futurism (in February 1908) Marinetti declared in his Futurist Manifesto: 'but we will hear no more about the past, we young strong Futurists'). It set up in our language or, if not set up, made febrile and judgemental such polarities as: 'progressive' and 'reactionary', 'forward-looking' and 'backward-looking', 'contemporary' and 'archaic', 'in fashion' and 'old-fashioned'/'out-dated'/'old-hat'.

Modernism is most characteristically described as a movement based on disruption, severance, a breaking with past practice. Defining Modernism in *The Oxford Companion to English Literature* Margaret Drabble wrote;

> Modernist literature is a literature of discontinuity both historically and aesthetically, being based upon a sharp rejection of the procedures and values of the immediate past, to which it adopts an adversarial stance.[3]

In a similar vein the Marxist critic Jurgen Habermas in an essay entitled *Modernity: an Incomplete Project* wrote:

> In the course of the 19th Century there emerged out of this Romantic spirit that radicalized consciousness of modernity which freed itself from all specific historical ties. This most recent Modernism simply makes an abstract opposition between tradition and the present; and we are in a way still the contemporaries of that kind of aesthetic modernity which first appeared in the midst of the 19th Century. Since then the distinguishing mark of works which count as modern is 'the new' which will be overcome and made obsolete through the novelty of the next style.[4]

The imperative is clear: obliterate the collective and historical memory. In this respect Modernism uncannily resembles certain elements in Progressive educational theory.

The very word 'progressive' has, indeed, that explosive word 'progress' at its centre. The last two meanings of the word progress given the Oxford English Dictionary are particularly pertinent: to make progress, to advance, get on; to develop; to improve continuously, to cause to advance; to push forward. A commitment to thrusting through space and time towards the next development would seem to mark out the commonground between the Modernist and the Progressivist. And yet in education the progressivist would tend to work with a different set of assumptions from the typical Modernist. He would invoke nature, biology, the innate unfolding of an inviolate identity. Progressive educators offer a country rhetoric, not a cosmopolitan one. The great inspiration and the major source of this movement remains Rousseau's *Emile*.

To achieve the ideal education Rousseau removed the child from the malign influences of civilization and placed him in the remote countryside. Emile was to grow up in and through communion with his own nature in relationship to Nature. 'In my view', Rousseau declared, 'everything ought to be in conformity with original inclinations', the innate inclinations of the body prior to the distorting influences of society. The progression, then, refers not to an inevitable historic unfolding but to the innate unfolding (without overt influence or formal restraint) of the interior nature of the individual child. Rousseau's ferocious attack on civilization and inherited culture is fallacious event if it remains truly eloquent:

> Man's wisdom is but servile prejudice; his customs but subjection and restraint. From the beginning to the end of life civilized man is a slave. At birth he is sewn up in swaddling bands and at death naileddown in a coffin. All through he is fettered by social institutions. Thus the internal impulses which should lead to growth find an insurmountable obstacle in the way of the necessary movements. The child exhausts his strength in vain struggles, or he gains strength very slowly. He was freer and less constrained in the womb; he has gained nothing by birth.[5]

So in this tradition progress tends to denote not the continuous advances of a Promethean civilization but the progressive unfolding of the unique individual removed from what are conceived as the falsifying influences of received traditions, spiritual, cultural, artistic. While Modernism and Progressivism have different starting points and concerns they yet both share a common disdain for the collective and historic past. In Rousseau's *Emile* nature is set up in opposition to civilization and interpreted as the justifying and primary category. In typical Modernism the past is seen as an impediment to expression and to the full and fitting response to the spirit of the age. 'Start from zero' urged Walter Gropius.

In our Century the two very complex movements come together in the figure and writing of Herbert Read. His volume, *Education Through Art* was his major contribution to educational theory. And it is to this book or rather one central chapter of this book that I now wish to turn.

The chapter is, significantly, titled *The Natural Form of Education* and, as significantly, quotes beneath its heading: 'remember that childhood is the sleep of reason', and exhortation from Rousseau. In this chapter Herbert Read offers his typology of arts teaching; he divides it into three areas; 'the activity of appreciation'. A good initial classification of tasks, one is tempted to say; but it is his interpretation of these three areas, informed by his progressivist notions of the child, which are of the greatest interest. First of all he states that each activity is best seen as a distinct subject, requiring separate and unrelated methods of approach. Then he comments of each activity in turn.

Of self-expression he writes that 'generally speaking' it 'cannot be taught'. Elaborating on this position he claims 'Any application of an external standard, whether of technique or form, immediately induces inhibitions, and frustrates the whole aim. The role of the teacher is that of attendant, guide, inspirer, psychic midwife'.

Observation, the second field of activity, in contrast is, according to Read, one that is almost entirely 'an acquired skill'. Having said it can be taught he then goes on to severely demote it:

> It is the usefulness of such acquired skill as an ancillary to the normal logical and scientific curriculum of the school which has led to the fanatical defence of naturalistic modes in art teaching, and a preference to 'craft' as opposed to art.

Then, finally, Herbert Read comments on appreciation. He insists that appreciation can be taught but, then goes on;

> But in so far as by appreciation we mean a response to other people's modes of expression.[6]

In brief, for Herbert Read - as for Rousseau - the essential task of the art teacher is to hold back the various conventions of the culture so that the children can naturally unfold out of their own uncorrupted natures. 'The adult's relation to the child', he wrote, 'must always be that of a collaborator never that of a master'. All that the teacher might formally introduce is devalued in comparison with what the child has to give to the teacher. This is child-centred education.

In Herbert Read I think it is possible to locate two main modern sources for the child-centred pedagogy. First there was his discovery of Carl Jung's writing on the collective unconscious, of a dynamic and creative conception of the psyche with its autonomous creativity. This promoted a view that interference from outside could only hinder or often distort the natural psychic process towards expressive symbolization. In *Education through Art*, Jung is quoted as saying 'Consciousness is for ever interfering, helping, correcting and negotiating, and never leaving the simple growth of psychic processes in peace'. In 1940 Herbert Read himself came across a drawing by a Cambridgeshire working-class girl aged five. It was called by the girl 'Snake round the World and a Boat'. (It is reproduced as figure 1b in *Education through Art*) According to Read it had been drawn by the child at home and was spontaneous in origin:

> I was deeply moved because what this child had drawn was one of the oldest symbols in the world - a magic circle divided into segments and known as the mandala, the symbol of the self as a psychic unity, a very ancient symbol found in Egypt and the Far East and throughout Europe in

the Middle Ages. This child of five had given me something in the nature of an apocalyptic experience.[7]

If so much was given by nature, what was the need for an inherited culture? Indeed, was there not the constant danger that any received culture would suppress the innate biological fund of symbolic images? From a different position, Rousseau's pedagogy was thus reaffirmed.

Read's growing commitment to the work of Jung and the notion of dynamic unconscious fused with those elements in Modernism which advocated a return to the immediate, the unpremeditated, the innocent. In *The Truth of a Few Simple Ideas*, Herbert Read tells us how in organizing some children's exhibitions abroad he met in Paris Picasso who, after examining the children's work, said: 'When I was the age of these children I could paid by Raphael. It took me many years to learn how to paint like these children'. For a moment the insights precipitated by child-art and those proclaimed by the avant-garde seemed to be identical. The aim thus became clear; it was to liberate the expressive impulse; to create an open space untouched by the images of Raphael or Rembrandt or, any previous art.

Similar versions of child-centred education, rooted often in further notions of 'play' deriving from psycho-analysis, can be found across the arts, particularly in the period between 1940 and 1970. It is strongly present in Drama which during this period disowned Theatre; it is present in Dance (particularly in the popularization of Laban's work) and, in a less focused and more diffused way, it can be discovered at work in Music and English teaching. What the believers in 'self-expression' valued was spontaneity, improvisation, originality, process; what was largely dismissed was the collective symbolic field in which the creation should have been taking place. There was little or no reference to achieved work in the artistic medium especially from the past few conventions, if any, were explicitly introduced. There was a general poverty of terms, critical and practical. What was missing in Iris Murdoch's language was 'the background' and the recognition of a wider order to which all the work produced belonged. The public nature of artistic production was entirely absent. There was no 'poetics' or 'rhetoric' to sustain, to extend, to connect the expressive act which grew repetitive and predictable from want of variety and outside challenge.

During this same period of progressive experimentation in education Modernism had entered its second and more negative phase. In *Living Powers*, I differentiated between the first vital movement of Modernism (1900-1940) and the second jaded movement of Late Modernism (1940-1980). I believe that the influences of Late Modernism and Progressivism working together, consciously and unconsciously, led to a state of severe symbolic depletion which most of us are now trying to recover from. We are now, almost by force of historic circumstance, cultural conservationists; not revolutionaries. What now could possibly be 'next' in any self-proclaimed artistic revolution? We now feel compelled to repair the lines that were broken off, to reestablish vital, though not necessarily uncritical, lines of communication with all that has gone before.

I would like to turn, finally, to Herbert Read's Modernism or, more precisely, his paradoxical attach on the 'achievements' of Modernism made at the end of his life. I say paradoxical because Read had been one of the greatest champions of artistic Modernism in Britain. It was as if in his last writing he was throwing his many manifestos into the fire as worthless prophecies, as proclamations of hope that could no longer withstand the test of passing time. It was as if Herbert Read in the last years of his life came to see many of the fruits of Modernism (and especially of Late Modernism) as withered and poisonous, as if he could sense some inversion at work in modern artistic expression but could not adequately locate its cause.

In 1962 in *What is There Left to Say*, Herbert Read had indicated his sense of isolation from his times. Commenting on the corroding cynicism and despair of most of the major authors of his period he wrote:

I was born with an innocence that is abashed by such cynicism, and for this reason alone I must retire into silence, or into the sacrificial busyness of committees.[8]

The paper ends with a dismissive reference to 'pop' artists and 'drug-addicts' and to the conclusion that the last phase of disintegration had set in. Yet in 1959 in a further preface to *Art Now*, Read had expounded in true Modernist style:

People forget that the artist (if he deserves that name) has the acutest sense of us all; and he can onlyby true to himself and to his function if he expresses that acuteness to the final edge. We are with courage, without freedom, without passion and joy, if we refuse to follow where he leads.[9]

Here we find the rhetorical assertion of the conception of the Avant-garde on which so many 'isms' of the 20th Century were to be quickly created and as quickly discarded. Yet Read's formulation is quintessentially vague. For what was 'the final edge' to which the artist was moving in 1959, just as the 60's were about to explode? And what was 'the final edge' to which many of the earlier Modernists had come? These are not speculative questions. They are the actual questions which Herbert Read came to ask himself in one of the last lecture he gave (on February 1st 1968, a few months before his death). And the answers he provided, as I will now briefly show, were as aesthetically critical as they were ethically bleak. They disclose, quite unambiguously, that Herbert Read had come to feel that 'the final edge' was not the right place for the arts to be.

Significantly, the lecture was entitled *The Limits of Permissiveness*.[10] He begins by defending the principle of Modernism and then plunges unexpectedly into the negative element. He attacks James Joyce's modernist masterpiece *Finnegans Wake*, quoting with approval Stanislaus' judgement that it represented 'the witless wandering of literature before its final extinction'. Its influence, he assets, 'has been disastrous'. He then moves onto damn the experimental work of Samuel Beckett. From 'a stylistic point of view, it has lead', he claims, 'to an apotheosis of futility' and to 'a permissive logorrhoea with so little aesthetic reward'. Having dismissed Beckett, he then dismisses the anti-novel of Alan Robbe-Grillet, Nathalie Sarraute and Marguerita Duras. They, he claims, have none of the movement, tension and resolution found 'in the great literature of the past'.

Next Herbert Read turns his critical eye on Ezra Pound and, while claiming that Pound must remain one of the great poets of our time, he goes on to quote with approval Yeat's judgement, referring to his 'nervous obsession', 'nightmare' and 'stammering confusion' Read concludes that, 'the stammering confusion has grown worse with every successive batch of cantos, until in the latest cantos the incoherence is absolute'. Of all Pound's disciples and imitators he declares that 'they mirror a great confusion and call it the modern style'.

After such a cursory and despairing evaluation of these major literary innovators and innovations, Read, the pioneer of cultural revolution, turns to the visual arts: 'I must now turn all too late in this lecture to the visual arts, for the process of disintegration is even more evident in painting and sculpture than in literature'. He praises the early work of the first Modernists : Picasso, Miro, Kandinsky, Henry Moore, but argues that the majority of those who had come to maturity after the Second World War (the period that I designate as that of Late Modernism) in their struggle to be original were 'compelled to deviate arbitrarily from the prototypes'. Earlier in the lecture Herbert Read had characterised the movement of Action Painting, Pop Art and Op Art as 'pseudo-movements . the creation of journalist . anxious to create an order where only confusion seems to exist'.

Read's extraordinary lecture finally ends with a plea that we reject 'contemporary nihilism in art' and 'withhold our approval from all those manifestations of permissiveness characterized by incoherence, insensibility, brutality and ironic detachment'. So much, then, for the artist having the acutest sense and for his audience following him to the final edge?

The Limits of Permissiveness is a moving, confused and disturbing document. It is permeated with a deep moral gloom and cultural apprehension. The despairing words; paranoia, confusion, incoherence, nihilism litter his text. Had the diverse phenomena of 'cultural nihilism' engendered in him a sense of deep cultural conservation? Certainly the reference to 'prototypes' and to 'the great literature of the past' imply both an enduring order greater than the modern and an aesthetic field of execution which, necessarily, transcended it.

Aware of the paradox of his own position as the pioneer of Modernism in art and of Progressivism in arts education, Herbert Read must have felt deeply uneasy. He saw the crisis. He sensed the subjective nihilism and the symbolic depletion. Yet, locked in his own progressive and modernist categories, perhaps he was not able to fully grasp the reasons for the collapse.

In the teaching of the arts I think we are responding to the extreme condition of social confusion half diagnosed by Herbert Read in his last lecture. We are also responding to the negative consequences of much progressive education, which also isolated from any common culture. It has been the burden of my argument that the related movements of Modernism and Progressivism were unable to provide an adequate or comprehensive aesthetic. The task now, in creative reaction, is to draw the public face of art and we must try and render it without losing the better insights of the better Modernists and Progressivists, for, surely we must still value experimentation in art and the individuality and spontaneity of each child? What is needed is not so much a reactive denial but a broader framework in which to work. I think that framework is now in the making.[11] I think it is prefigured in the quotation from Iris Murdoch with which I began.

NOTES AND REFERENCES

1. Iris Murdoch, 'Against Dryness a Polemical Sketch' First published in *Encounter* January 1961
2. Ernst Gombrich in *Tributes:* Interpretations of our Cultural History (Phaidon 1984) p.89
3. Margaret Drabble, *The Oxford Companion to English Literature* (new Edition 1985)
4. Jurgen Habermas, 'Modernity: an Incomplete Project' in *Post-Modern Culture* ed. Hal Foster (Pluto Press 1983) p.4.
5. Jean Jacques Rousseau from *Emile*, first published in 1762. Translated by Barbara Foxley. Everyman Edition 1911 pp.10-1
6. Herbert Read, *Education through Art* (Faber and Faber Third Edition 1956) p.209
7. Herbert Read, 'The Truth of a Few Simple Ideas' in *The Cult of Sincerity* (Faber and Faber 1968) p.45
8. Herbert Read, 'What is There Left to Say?' in *The Cult of Sincerity, ibid* p.57
9. Herbert Read, *Art Now* (Faber and Faber 1933) Preface to the Revised Edition 1960, p.11
10. *The Limits of Permissiveness* is published in The Black Rainbow: Essays on the Present Breakdown of Culture ed. Peter Abbs (Heinemann Educational Books 1975)
11. In particular it is the philosophical framework which unifies the current Falmer Press Library on Aesthetic Education which will represent each of the major arts disciplines, Art, Drama, Dance, Music, Literature and Film as member of a single generic family within the curriculum.

CULTURE AND THE ARTS

PROFESSOR JOHN BLACKING, QUEENS UNIVERSITY, BELFAST

Since I shall discuss the arts in a so-called multicultural society, I will first make clear the distinction between general and restricted uses of the word 'culture'.

The word 'culture' is used to refer specifically to the arts, and more generally to the distinctive ways of life which all people share by virtue of being human. Confusion of the two uses of the word 'culture' can lead to misunderstanding of the roles of the arts and of culture in people's individual development.

For instance, Article 27 of the *Universal Declaration of Human Rights* states a general principle and then uses 'culture' in a limited sense: it declares that 'everyone has the right freely to participate in the cultural life of the community, to enjoy the arts and to share in scientific achievement and its benefits'. Perhaps as a consequence of this, 'culture' is used in both ways as important UNESCO reports on people's participation in cultural life (1976), on the status of the artists (1980), and on cultural policies in general (1982). As a result, they convey the impression that artists are the 'creators and bearers of cultural values' (UNESCO 1976:2), and that culture is something that people receive, or not, rather than something that all human beings acquire and go on inventing and re-making as long as they exercise their innate human capacities in the course of social interaction.

Culture, in the general sense of the life-style of a community, is performed and exists only in performance, no less than does culture in the limited sense of the arts. Cultures are products of human individuation, and they are re-interpreted, translated, by every individual and every generation. Cultural variety does not have to be nurtured: it is an inevitable outcome of human sociability and creativity. What does have to be cultivated is an environment in which people can grow and interact. When this is neglected, in an economically and socially divided community, 'the agonistic functions of speech outweigh the functions of genuine communication social classes, racial ghettos speak at rather than to each other' (Steiner 1975: 32).

One of the most terrifying consequences of the development in material culture and technology of the past two centuries is that they have made possible the concentration of wealth and authoritarian power in the hands of tiny minorities of people. The failure of human beings to develop their non-material culture as efficiently as their technology and techniques of communication is a major problem of the modern world. It has alienated millions of people and driven them to look back to a past that was in many respects no better, in desperate attempts to adapt to and re-educate themselves for contemporary evolutionary challenges.

In this process, people become deeply attached to cultures and a sense of 'cultural identity', as if cultural systems had intrinsic value as permanent solutions to the problems of living, and as if cultures, and not individuals, were sources of the imagination and invention which are always necessary to solve the recurring problems of relationships and institutional organisation that hinder human development. Cultural chauvinism is usually a response to oppression and persecution, rather than a psychological necessity.

Thus people often leave a country because its cultural system is deficient and restricts their 'self-actualization'. The, because the social system of their country of adoption is also deficient and they feel ill at ease, or superior, or oppressed in some way, they try to re-create for their children elements of their original life style. These may be inappropriate in the new context, and hence restrict rather than nourish their natural creativity and adaptability. Co-operation and continuous education in a social context are conditions of becoming human, but when the common humanity is redefined as members of a particular society or subscribers to a particular cultural system, human energy and creativity are misapplied.

Insofar as the arts are part of the general culture of different societies, 'every work of art is a simplification of the whole complexity of reality based on convention in accordance with the interests of the particular social class that created it' (Berger 1972: 215). The value of the arts in any society rests ultimately on the kind of quality of human experiences that are invoked in their creation, performance, and evaluation. They can be used as symbolic objects whose form is related to their use solely by decree.

For instance, a piece of music may be declared political or typical of a particular ethnic group, and used as such without regard to its musical content. Any shared symbol-system can be a basis for human communication and so artists could be described as creators and performers of totemic rites and objects whose value lies in the social solidarity and sense of well being that people derive simply from coming together with a common purpose. What participants share is the special knowledge of a self-selected class of people; expansion of that knowledge is chiefly in the interests of the spread of influence of the groups who control and identify themselves with the knowledge. It must be understood that Shakespeare, Bach and Bharata Natyam can be treated in this way no less than football, country music, and disco-dancing. 'High Art' is not automatically more worthy than 'low art': appreciation of Beethoven's music did not restrain the jailers of Auschwitz.

Thus the arts can serve oppressors as well as help the liberation of the oppressed (cf. Tax 1972). Similarly, cultural systems cannot be accepted uncritically as inherently good. Whole societies or parts of a society can become dangerous deviant, as were Nazi society and the Khmer Rouge. In this respect there is a serious contradiction in the UNESCO resolutions about culture and their condemnation of Israel and South Africa. If 'the equal dignity of cultures must be recognised as an inviolable principle' (UNESCO 1982:189), there are no grounds for condemning apartheid. Cultures must always be under critical review. Cultural relativism is a well intentioned but essentially false doctrine that can blind us to the fact that societies can become pathological, and that too much emphasis on cultural identity, as distinct from personal identity and self-actualisation, can hasten the process. Policies of asserting cultural identity, if taken to extremes, can lead to racism and fascism. Culture has been defined as 'that complex whole which includes knowledge, belief, art, morals, law, custom, and any other capabilities and habits acquired by man as a member of a group' (Tylor 1871:1).

The concept of culture is an abstraction designed to describe all the patterns of thought and interaction that persist in communities over time. We cannot 'see' a culture: we can only infer its existence from regularities in the form of distribution of events and objects that we observe.

Cultures are the experiments which human communities have devised at different times and in different places not only to get a material living, but above all to provide a framework for making sense of profound emotions, institutionalising love and the joy of association, and finding new ways of extending the body. Cultural systems have not always succeeded in providing the means for all members of a society to live freely and at ease to realise their full potential, or for a society to live in peace with its neighbours.

The arts are part of the general culture of a group. As symbolic objects, they may be socially useful, but it cannot be argued that they have any special value. But as symbol systems whose 'performance' is the chief reason for their existence, they can have profound effects on individual consciousness, which in turn can affect people's imagination and decision making in other social contexts.

In many African societies, the arts have been and are seen not merely as part of the superstructure of human life, as optional extras that can be added, when there is an economic surplus, for entertainment and refreshment or for reinforcing the power of certain social groups. They have been regarded as integral parts of societies' processes of reproduction and material production, as means of defining self and others and the conditions of sharing that are necessary for the welfare and economic success of communities (Blacking 1973:101).

In the UNESCO resolutions to which I have referred, member states have agreed in principle that the arts must have a central role within the development process as a whole (UNESCO 1982:189). There is no doubt about the importance of the arts in pre-industrial societies, where the division of labour, international capitalism and monopolies of power and wealth, and the mobility of populations seeking work and escaping from poverty, have reached crisis proportions.

One of the responses to this crisis has been to emphasise the cultural identity of oppressed or minority groups as part of political and educational campaigns to improve their condition. In certain circumstances this can be a necessary phase in the liberation of a community or nation. But in other situations, such a response can enslave people in the irrelevance of searching for cultural identity, instead of the means of personal freedom. An example of this was the South African policy of separate development which was first devised by a well-meaning

84

academic, Professor Werner Eislen, as a solution to what he saw as the decline and decay of African cultures.

We must not forget that a policy of multicultural education was one of the corner-stones of apartheid, and that many of the arguments in its favour were similar to those heard in the United Kingdom in recent years!

If we take the limited definition of culture as the arts, it need hardly be said that almost every society is 'multicultural', in the sense that its people generate a variety of artistic styles. The argument is not worth pursuing, and so I will consider the notion that some societies and multicultural in the sense that their citizens pursue different and distinctive ways of life. It has become fashionable to describe the United Kingdom as 'a multicultural society', as if the phrase described a new condition. In one sense, it has been a multicultural society since 1066 and before, and this is reflected in the English language. We refer to meat when it is served at table by words that are French in origin: beef, mutton, and pork. But the animals that provide meat are called by the Anglo-Saxon words used by the serfs that looked after them: ox, sheep, and pig. Since the Act of Union, the United Kingdom has incorporated people of four nationalities that might be described as having distinct cultures: English, Welsh, Scottish and Irish. Furthermore, there are great differences between the life-styles and values of the friendly people of the north of England and the natives of the south-eastern stockbroker belt; between different social classes; between art worlds; business worlds, and agricultural worlds: and between fundamentally different types of Jewish and Christian denomination.

Current rhetoric about 'multiculturalism' tends to ignore these deeply rooted differences in the cultures of natives of the UK whose families have lived in the country for generations. Implicitly, and often explicitly, the concept is used to refer to the different life-styles of British citizens whose ancestors were reared in the Caribbean, South and East Asia, Eastern Europe, and the Mediterranean, partly because their families settled in the country comparatively recently, but chiefly because most of them are considered to be racially different and not all of them speak English. It matters little that Indians, Pakistanis, Bangladeshis, Cypriots and Italians all belong biologically to the same race as the majority of British citizens: Caucasiform or Caucasoid. The trouble is that people believe that they are racially different because of variations in hair and skin colour. It matters little that even the most extreme physical differences of the human species are accounted for by less than 5% of our genetic make-up and that in all other respects the differences among two 'white' Englishmen and two 'black' Ghanaians could be greater than the differences between a Ghanaian and an Englishman. Many people believe that there are fundamental differences of character, intellect and morality which spring from racial differences.

The presence of these mistaken beliefs in the United Kingdom is the result of the appalling failure of British civil and religious education, and it should be a source of national shame. The most important issues in British education and in British society are not economic. It is not an economy which keeps a society together, but good social relations which bring societies into existence and make economies possible. The most important issues in British education and in British society are therefore social, and they are most apparent in class distinction, social inequality, and racism. These are central issues that have led to a concern with so-called 'multicultural' education and I shall return to them.

But before doing so I want to reiterate my points about the multicultural character of British society. The cultural differences among English speaking Christians whose families have lived in England for at least eight generations can be as great as the differences between white English speaking families and first and second generation families of Gujarati-speaking Hindus or Urdu-speaking Moslems. The differences between different white English people are minimised and those between English and others are emphasised, partly because it is politically expedient to do so, and partly because differences in racial type, language, and religion are more easily marked. But race and language are not necessarily coterminous with culture, and religion is only one aspect of a cultural system. Moreover, although Islam may appear monolithic to many English Christians, the divisions within it are as great as the divisions within Christianity.

If there is such a phenomenon as a British national character, there is a sense in which it has been 'multicultural' for at least 500 years. It has been deeply affected by the colonial experience. The 'British' national drink is tea, first grown in China. Many British men and women wear pyjamas at night, an idea from India. We consume vast quantities of sugar, originally from Jamaica and the Caribbean, and cocoa brought from Mexico via Spain. We also drink a great deal of coffee, which was grown by Arabs near the Red Sea and brought to Europe in the 17th Century. I need hardly say how our diet has been enriched by Chinese and Indian food, and how many characteristically British dishes are colonial in origin, such as the Kedgeree that we had at my school, and the rice pudding. The English Language is full of words of Asian and African origin. British domestic furniture has been profoundly influenced by Asian styles and practice. Even an interest in Eastern religions is the result not of immigration, but of British citizens coming home after periods of foreign service in the army, the civil service, or some firm. For example, the first British mosque was built in Woking in 1889 not for Pakistani or Arab immigrants, but for English people returning from India, where they had been influenced by Islam. It was largely financed by the Begum Shah Jehan, after whom it is called.

Thus it is not African, Asian and Caribbean immigrants who were in the first place responsible for making the UK a 'multicultural society'. The seeds were sown long before they arrived. What their presence has done is to confront UK citizens with the domestic roots of the cultures whose products they already adopted or enjoyed, and with the fact that they were created by different 'ethnic' or racial groups. Above all, what was at first a process of easy assimilation became a process of separation and antagonism. Studying Hinduism and eating curry, enjoying jazz and Chinese pottery and African sculpture, did not at first require close association with the inventors of those cultural traits. And when immigrants from India, the Caribbean, Hong Kong and Africa did come to the

UK in large numbers, most of them came as low-paid workers and many lacked the cultural refinements which had been admired.

What is now often defined as a conflict of cultures within the UK is really the result of British racism and of the failure of successive governments to ensure that all immigrants had adequate opportunities to learn the English Language, and to acquire expertise in dealing with bureaucracy, the law, local customs, and so on. It is still not too late to invest in special 'initiation schools' which would help immigrants to become skilled in coping with their new home; but we seem to be side-stepping the real issues of effective incorporation and equality of opportunity in what is in fact a monocultural state and education system by promoting the white South African 'solution' of separatism or 'multiculturalism'.

The cultural stereotypes that are in danger of being enshrined by the current rhetoric and action of 'multicultural education' could have detrimental effects on the development of individuals in the very communities which the policies are designed to help. For example, 'black issues' have become race relations and culture, but not defence and economy, and the sharing of power. The music of immigrants has become 'ethnic' music, a spurious category which insults the creators of the music and ignores the fact that Indian music, African music, Balinese music, etc are, like European music, created not by some amorphous collective, but by individual composers and performers who are known and recognised in their communities as were Bach in Leipzig, Beethoven in Bonn, and Schubert in Vienna. People and artistic traditions have been re-classified in curious ways: learning 'African' music has come to mean learning one or two genres of Ghanaian music; and although the term 'Afro-Caribbean' underlines the common experience of colonialism and may be useful for political activism in the United Kingdom, it effectively denies the uniqueness and inventiveness of Caribbean societies and the diversity and the history of African societies. Similarly, Steel Band music and Reggae seem to have been given the status of traditional music, whereas they were invented in the 1940s and 1950s respectively, and are considerably younger than the Tango and Jazz. Moreover, Reggae is only one of several Jamaican music styles, and it does Jamaican musicians a disservice to imply that it is the music of Jamaica.

I shall return to the problem of presenting work of African, Asian and Caribbean artist in the United Kingdom when I discuss arts education. In summing up this section, I want to agree with Professor John Rex that the United Kingdom is not 'and is unlikely to become a multicultural society in the sense that Brussels is. There two ethnic groups actually share political power and their languages may equally be used in parliament and the Civil Service' (Swann 1985:240). On the other hand, it is a fact that many aspects of its social and domestic life, England in particular has been 'multicultural' for at least 900 years. What has happened in the last forty years, and what makes radical changes in education imperative, is that the racism that has always been latent in British society is no longer tucked away in the colonies. It has become a major factor in the corruption and decay of the United Kingdom. There is not a multicultural society so much as a deeply divided society. What is needed first is the systematic undoing of racism in ways that are as effective as was the anti-slavery campaign in the first quarter of the nineteenth century.

In my view, the educational solutions to these problems are neither 'multicultural' education nor emphasis on the United Kingdom as a 'multicultural' society. The United Kingdom is a racist society and all its citizens need anti-racist education that respects the cultural achievements of individuals in all parts of the world.

Anti-Racist Education

The Centre for Multicultural Education published a working paper on Race Education and Research: Rampton, Swann and after, in 1984. Its authors were apprehensive that the final report of the Swann Committee of Inquiry into the Education of Ethnic Minority Groups would fail to tackle issues of race and the overall structure of British society, and would seek to explain the apparently poor academic performance of many children in terms of inadequate family background, language disabilities, and so on. It seemed to me, on reading the final Swann Report, that the Committee had in fact faced this problem, and had produced an important series of recommendations. I will summarise them briefly, as I understand them:

They recognised that schools must play a leading role in changing behaviour and attitudes towards ethnic minorities, and that 'the fundamental change that is necessary is the recognition that the problem facing the education system is not how to educate children of ethnic minorities, but how to educate all children' (Swann 1985:769, 3.1 (a)): 'it is necessary to combat racism, to attack inherited myths and stereotypes and the ways in which they are embodied in institutional practices' (3.1 (e)). 'Multicultural understanding has also to permeate all aspects of a school's work. It is not a separate topic that can be welded on to existing practices' (3.1(f)). 'Only in this way can schools begin to offer anything approaching the equality of opportunity for all pupils which it must be the aspiration of the education system to provide' (3.1(g)).

The report concluded that there is a dual problem of 'eradicating the discriminatory attitudes of the white minority on the one hand, and on the other, evolving an education system which ensures that all pupils achieve their full potential (2.6, p. 768). 'Examining Boards should reflect cultural diversity in the syllabuses they offer and in their working practice' (4.7, p.770); they should 'broaden the school curriculum'.

The members of the Committee came out strongly against separatism in education and in favour of English as the language of instruction; but they argued that 'LEAs should offer support for community based language provision' (5.9, p.772), and that in certain areas 'ethnic minority community languages should be included in the language curriculum of secondary schools' (5.10, p.772), in the same way that French and German are offered.

My only strong opposition to the recommendations is directed at their plea for the collection of 'ethnically-based educational statistics' (pp.xxiii xxiv and 775). I regard this as a retrograde step reminiscent of the South African

Population Registration Act and wholly out of keeping with the high-minded aims of *Education for All*. In social matters, statistics are seldom used to anyone's advantage; and the recent ESRC hit-list of tertiary institutions is a classic example of how phoney statistics can be meretriciously used to avoid the effort of tackling a serious problem. We must stop using terms like 'ethnic minority', or cultural group - especially in the arts. As part of the campaign against racism, we must abolish all census figures that identify race, religion, or ethnic minority affiliation. What matters in educational development is whether or not all British Citizens are being properly educated.

A sentence in the Swann Report is typical of the kind of attitude that can be too easily accepted when ethnic and cultural identities are emphasised. A section of a research report on a school began: 'this large co-educational comprehensive school had a substantial group of Italian pupils many of whom were third generation "immigrants" ' (Swann 1985: 254). It is clearly nonsense to refer to those pupils as Italians, as it often is to refer to other British citizens as Indians, Pakistanis or West Indians.

My objection to 'ethnic' statistics does not include all kinds of 'ethnic monitoring'. For example, I accept as timely and necessary a study such as that by Cecil Wright on white teachers' discrimination against 'West Indian' school children (Wright 1985A), and more of this kind of evidence is needed. At the same time, we must recognise that discrimination also occurs in all-white schools. It happened at both my schools, and not only to Irish boys: there was, for instance, one boy who was constantly attacked by his teachers and who often responded in the same rebellious ways as Cecil Wright's subjects. He is now a successful businessman and Tory MP, with strong views on law and order! I can also accept the need for limited amount of 'ethnic' statistics in research studies of particular schools (eg. Wright 1985B), but I can see no need for any more general statistics. The fact about the educational performance are known, the racism is there and acknowledged, and no amount of statistics will help us to combat it. If research is really needed to plan action which to me seems so obvious that it needs no further research, the most useful approach would be detailed analyses of classroom interaction, and especially of teachers' attitudes and pupils' intelligent responses. There is real danger, too, that 'ethnic' statistics can mask important factors which cut across ethnic boundaries, such as social deprivation and poverty.

People should resist ethnically-based educational statistics as strongly as South African Blacks object to being classified according to tribal identities which could expedite removal to a Bantustan and deprive them of their South African passports. White South Africans viewed blacks not as free-thinking individuals but as products of some kind of cultural machine. It was, in fact, the whites who were obsessed with culture.

The Venda of the Northern Transvaal, on the other hand, were typical of many African societies whose members were not greatly concerned with the preservation or promotion of their culture. Their indigenous education system, informal and formal, was directed towards the maintenance of general human values and of an open society whose political economy allowed individuals to flourish and use their innate creative capacities for their own self-satisfaction and the benefit of the community at large. They used dances, songs, music, mimes and myth to impart values to ensure people's security. But they were not ends in themselves except insofar that some performances helped to generate the transcendental experiences that proved to individual Venda the reality of the spiritual self, which was the link between the eternal world of nature and the ancestral spirits and the transitory cultural forms of the contemporary society.

In other words, the Venda did not see culture as something fixed and immutable. It was, rather, a floating resource which was available for use, or not, as part of the process of developing human capabilities through social interaction, sharing ideas and learning skills. Just as people took what they wanted from available Venda institutions and ideas, so they also sought 'Western' education as a means of fulfilment and of escaping from the oppression of apartheid:they took it for granted that the history, political science, and religious education would be ethnocentric; but they valued instruction in 'universal' skills such as medicine, mathematics, chemistry, and engineering. They saw education, as a deliberate attempt to suppress their talents and social mobility.

I have already mentioned that one of the problems about the idea of multicultural education is its misrepresentation of the concept of culture. Strictly speaking, 'multicultural education' must mean separate education, because different systems of education cannot be combined; that is, the distinctiveness of each cultural system is automatically eliminated as soon as they are presented within a single educational system. One can, for instance, teach French or Greek history within the British educational system, and one can teach about French or Greek culture. But this does not make it multicultural education. It remains British education, geared towards a particular technology, particular means of production, power systems and political formations. If the concept of 'multicultural education' is to be correctly applied, people from different cultural backgrounds must be educated in ways appropriate to their cultures. Thus people of Pakistan, Indian and Caribbean origin living in England should be educated as if they were going to live in Pakistan, India, or the Caribbean. This might be appropriate if they were planning to return soon to those countries or to live in ghettos in the United Kingdom. But if they are to be active citizens of the United Kingdom, it is putting them at a disadvantage, in much the same way that segregated Bantu Education restricted the development of South African Blacks.

In any case, it is not the business of British schools to prepare children for life in Pakistan or the Punjab any more that it was their business to prepare my grandmother to return to the Warsaw ghetto or my children to go to Gujerat, from where my wife's father's family originated. But it is their business to prepare them for full participation in the social, economic, political and artistic life of the United Kingdom and of the world at large.

When there is talk of a multicultural society, we need to know what are the political motives for denying that a state is effectively monocultural, or that at least the subscribers to the dominant cultural systems intend to maintain their hegemony over others. In many cases a stated concern for the political promotion of culture is an evasion or denial of the real issues of equality of power, wealth and personal opportunity, combined with the common misconception of culture as something fixed or static, and the failure to recognise the innate intelligence and potential of ordinary human beings.

When we emphasise people's ethnic or cultural allegiances as a basis for association, learning and action, we generally deny some of their rights as persons. If the term 'multicultural society' helps us to appreciate more keenly the cultures of wealth and poverty, class and religion, occupation and unemployment, equality and inequality, maleness and femaleness, adulthood and childhood, then it could sensitise us to the problems and responsibilities of developing human resources in every part of the world. But if the concept of a multicultural society becomes a platform for a policy of identifying sections of national populations in terms of their countries of origin, and promoting contextless and often outmoded cultural traditions it can only create serious problems of identity and division within a generation, and in the United Kingdom could easily transplant the ancient rivalries, tensions and contests of Europe and Asia to a country which already has enough of its own social and cultural problems.

Anti-racist education requires that all British citizens receive the same basic education in one of the world's Great Traditions, a civilisation that followed on from those of Africa and Asia and happens to be influential in the world at the moment. It must not be associated specifically with ethnic groups of European origin. It is, in fact, an amalgam of the inventions and ideas of individuals from Egypt, Iraq, China, India, Indonesia, Persia, the Danube Valley, Greece, Rome, West Africa and other parts of the world.

Unfortunately, Europeans failed to spread this tradition amongst themselves, because they became bogged down in futile power struggles, violence, and cultures, of inequality. But from the rubble some products have remained for all, such as the work of Plato, Aristotle, Europides, Shakespeare, Virgil, Bramante, Michelangelo, Bach, Beethoven, Darwin, Einstein, and many other individuals.

The Great Tradition of Europe must remain at the core of formal education in the United Kingdom, because it has been developed in Europe and is appropriate for that environment. Not only should its African and Asian origins be recognised, but the core of African and Asian Great Traditions should be taught in the context of the European Great Tradition, and not as some marginal concern in the interests of a 'multicultural' perspective.

This there is not simply a problem of adding new items to existing syllabus as a sop to the presence of people of African, Asian and Caribbean origin. The whole way of presenting the European tradition must be radically altered, as it was at the time of the Renaissance. The outlook must be global. As Greece and Rome were brought into orbit of European learning so now we must bring in the cultural achievements of artists, scholars, scientists, engineers, architects and creative individuals and schools from Asia, Africa and other parts of the world.

I have searched in vain for signs of this change of direction in the 'O' and 'A' level syllabuses. It seems to me that they remain as myopic and Eurocentric as ever, and even fail to take account of the influences of the Islamic world on European music and architecture, of Japanese, Chinese and African art on European painting and sculpture and so on. One would at least have thought it appropriate to have given more than a cursory glance at the cultures and histories of the societies which were at the receiving end of Britain's colonial, industrial and commercial enterprises. The Swann Report has insisted that a change should be made in syllabuses and examinations, as part of the programme to combat racism. But what do we find? 'Composers of Western Europe', 'History of European Architecture', 'Macmillan, Fokine, Petipa, Davies' the litany of topics betrays a narrow definition of the words Art, Music, Dance, Literature, that is quite out of touch with the realities of the modern world.

Insofar as culture might be invoked in educational strategies that should be primarily anti-racist, Paulo Freire's concept of 'cultural synthesis' is probably the most appropriate. In his book, *Pedagogy of the Oppressed*, he contrasts this with 'cultural invasion', in which the actors 'superimpose themselves on the people who are assigned to the role of spectators of objects. In cultural synthesis, the actors become integrated with the people, who are the co-authors of the actions that both perform on the world. In cultural synthesis there are no invaders; hence there are no imposed models. In their stead, there are actors who critically analyse reality (never separating this analysis from action) and intervene as subjects in the historical process' (Freire 1979:783).

The Scope Of Arts Education

Freire's words lead on directly to two main principles that should guide arts education in the UK:

1. Because art does not reside in objects but in the ways that human beings make sense of the world, education in the arts must be concerned with the development of every citizen's artistic capabilities, and not only with the vocational training of artists.

2. In the contemporary world, and particularly in a country like the United Kingdom where anti-racist education is essential, arts education must be world arts education, and the emphasis must be on the contributions of individuals. The arts must not be betrayed to the interests of cultural hegemony.

Cultures are not sacrosanct, but the arts may be. For example, the fact that Richard Strauss wrote *Capriccio* during the Nazi period and that he seems to have had an ambivalent attitude to the regime should not interfere with our appreciation of this marvellous opera.

The notion of multiculturalism in the arts education implicitly denies both the individuality and transcendental universality of the arts. It is as unhelpful to say that Wagner and Strauss were products of German culture as it was arrogant of German missionaries to think they were intellectually and morally superior to their African neighbours because undoubtedly great individuals like Bach, Beethoven, Goethe, and Schiller happened to have been Germans. The absurdity of 'multicultural' arts education was brought home to me forcibly when an African scholar complained about the captions to some of my photographs of Venda musicians. 'How would you react to portraits of Bach, Mozart or Litzt', he said, 'if the captions read: "A German musician playing a two-manual organ", "An Austrian composer", or "A Hungarian playing the piano"?'

The arts are essentially about aesthetic experiences and the creative expression of individual human beings in community, about the sharing of feelings and ideas. Many musicians have composed for their loved ones, their own friends, and their own musical groups or religious congregations. They were not greatly concerned with nations and ethnic groups, except when they were exiled or when national themes and interests were fashionable: artificial boundaries were inimical to the spirit of art and human brotherhood. The purpose of arts education should be to help individuals to develop their aesthetic experience and understanding by exercising their powers of discrimination.

How art forms are presented is no less important than what is offered. In expanding the range of British arts education, it is not just a question of what we can bring in from India or the Caribbean? But how can we combat narrowmindedness, racism, prejudice in school books, and ethnocentricism in education? How can we teach people through artistic praxis that there is a larger social world outside and a richer world of experience inside each individual? If British arts education is to reflect a 'multicultural' society, its task is not so much to make blacks feel at home in school, as to make sure that white children are really aware of the historical and cultural traditions of their black neighbours. For instance, in order to counteract ethnocentric and derogatory classifications of music (e.g. Bach, Beethoven, Mozart, Debussy, Duke Ellington etc versus 'ethnic' music), emphasis must be laid on the contributions of individual composers and performers. Education authorities must ensure that schools have visits and workshops by highly skilled performers of compositions and genres that have been developed in Asia and Africa, as well as by pianists and violinists. It is necessary for children to hear a piano recital by a Jamaican or an Indian and a sitar recital by an English person, if only to demonstrate the individuality and transcendental universality of the arts.

The aim of arts in schools must not be to reinforce tribal boundaries and cultural stereotypes or to encourage tokenism by concentrating on pop music in predominantly 'working class' schools, reggae in schools with children of Caribbean origin, or Urdu folksongs where there are majorities of Pakistanis. It is not the business of arts educators to subvent community activities, which already exist, or to encourage cultural brokers to mobilise new social groups for social, political or religious purposes. Arts education should not be used to emphasise culture, because as soon as that happens there arise arguments about cultural hegemony, as well as false notions of what culture is: it should emphasise human variety and ingenuity. Arts education should not be cosy or comfortable; for the arts as passive entertainment, or as sensuous gratification of totemic identities; are invariably corrupting. It is the business of arts educators to induce in all their pupils new artistic experiences, which may or may not generate new social experiences. Their task is not simply to train professional artists, but to raise the general artistic consciousness of the masses to heights of professional excellence.

Since contemporary British society is in certain respects 'multicultural' and has been so for several centuries, the introduction of the serious study of world of arts in schools could be a distinctive British characteristic of arts education in the United Kingdom: it would recognise the varied cultural origins of the country's citizens and the many life-styles that coexist, while at the same time stimulating a sense of national unity by means of the common interest in artistic exploration and experience. The presence of the African and Asian arts has value in the context of the European Great Tradition because they are novel and technically different systems. If, however, they are promoted for social reasons, simply because there are persons of African and Asian origin living in the country, their value is immediately debased. In effect, they would be re-classified as a Little Tradition of Europe, and the opportunity of fruitful dialogue with the Great Traditions of Africa and Asia would thereby be lost development of arts education in schools has created new contexts for all kinds of artistic activity. Neither British folk arts nor Pakistani, Indian and Caribbean arts can be taught or presented in 'the appropriate cultural context'. But there are important ways in which they can be learnt out of context. There is no contradiction in the idea of teaching World Arts to promote national unity. An emphasis on individual creators and performers, and a global view of the artistic conventions that they have used and use, are the surest means of developing the artistic consciousness of the nation in ways that will help to adapt and strengthen 'the British character' for life in the 21st century. Of course, it requires an act of faith in the power of artistic symbols. Such as an enterprise will never succeed if it is multicultural: it must be multiartistic. It can only be successful when people are touched by the aesthetic force of the arts and can transcend their social and cultural analogues. A policy of teaching the best of the world's arts, as well as those of the European tradition, both includes the heritage of members of the new British nation and looks forward and outward to parts of the world that have not be specially involved in the British experience. Clearly not everything can or should be taught, and the syllabus must be selective as well as representative.

The argument that syllabuses are already too full cannot be sustained. For example, in music there are dozens of European composers whose work is completely absent from the present syllabus, as well as many masterpieces of the old favourites. It has generally been accepted that a study of two or three key words of a period is sufficient to illustrate general principles that can subsequently be applied by students in private study; and the same system of teaching can be extended to the music of other periods and places. Furthermore, the study of Asian and African musics raises interesting issues about the parameters that are currently used (e.g. tonality, rhythm, etc) and the ways in which they are presented, and suggests that there may be more parsimonious and effective ways of analysing all musics. The point is that the study of European music has much to gain technically from being conducted within the broader framework of World Musics. And I am sure that the same will apply to the teaching of other art forms.

I will conclude by repeating some remarks which I made in a publication on 'multicultural' music education, from which I have quoted without acknowledgement in this paper.

> Hitherto, what Europe has learnt from Asia has become part of the European Great Tradition, and what Asia has learnt from Europe has become part of Indian, Chinese, Japanese, or Indonesian Great Traditions. It is not the task of formal education systems to transmit Little Traditions, as distinct from knowledge about them and awareness of their presence. In the context of contemporary British society, Indipop clearly has more significance that Khyal or Kathak, and a policy of multicultural education could entrench this division. With an open-minded system of World music education appropriate for the Great Tradition of Europe, Kyal and Kathak, as well as Indipop, would receive proper attention, not because there are British citizens of Indian origin living in the United Kingdom, but because these artistic styles should be valued in their own right, as products of one of the Great Traditions of the World. (Blacking)

NOTES

1.   There are some useful points in Verity Saifullah Khan's (1985) critique of chapter 7 on *Language and Language Education*, but their impact is dimished by unreasonable accusations of dishonesty and racism (especially pp. 15 and 26) on the part of the Committee which really cannot be supported by a careful reading of the report as a whole. It seems to me that several other critisms of the Report have been based on reading only parts of it, or worse still, only Lord Swann's personal summary.

2.   The tasks of transmitting elements of a cultural tradition formally at school are quite different from those of transmitting the domestic and religious traditions of the home and the neighbourhood. There is a very real sense in which schools should not be like homes, and most children are the first to appreciate this and thrive on it. They systematically adopt different strategies at home and at school, and the tension between the two is probably a source of creative imagination. This is not a peculiarly 'Western' phenomenen or a peculiar product of industrial societies. For instance, the notion of forming schooling as strange, different, expansive, was enshrined in the traditional Southern African systems of education which I studied. Young people wanted to go to initiation schools to learn something new, new songs and dances and esoteric knowledge.

3.   I have, for instance, encountered cultural stereotypes in the teaching of African music, which emphasise popular misconceptions about drumming. Most people trained in a European musical tradition tend to emphasise its rhythmic

characteristics or the 'messages' that the drums can transmit (thus confusing the uses of drums as music, as poetry, and as a sort of Morse Code.) Anyone who spends time in Africa and learns from African musicians will soon find that drums are invariably perceived as melodic instruments, and 'polyrhythms' as polyphonic counterpoint. These are important musical conventions that must be understood if performances of African music are to have value in music education. It is possible for UK citizens of Caribbean and African origin to hear and interpret African music in an unAfrican way, as indeed many Western-educated Africans have misunderstood the traditional music of their own countries. I have attended classes and performances of African music in the United Kingdom where the subleties and gentle beauty of the music are suppressed by an emphasis on noise and rhythm and a Boy-Scout-camp attitude to performance. African music is often popular, in the sense that everyone in the community appreciates it and most people like to participate in performance; but the ethos of much African traditional music is 'classical', and it should be treated as seriously as the music of Bach and Mozart and Beethoven.

REFERENCES

Berger, John (1972), 'Problems in socialist art.' Lee Baxandall(ed.), *Radical Perspectives in the Arts*, Harmondsworth: Penguin, pp.209-224.
Blacking, John (1973), *How Musical is Man?* Seattle: University of Washington Press.
Blacking, John(1985), 'A False Trail for the Arts?' 'Multicultural' Music Education and the denial of individual creativity. In Malcolm Ross (ed.), *The Aesthetic in Education*, Oxford: Pergamon Press, pp. 1-27.
Centres for Multicultural Education (1984), Race, education and Research: *Rampton, Swann and after.* Working Paper No.3., London Institute of Education.
Freire, Paulo (1979), *Pedagogy of the Oppressed*, tr. Myra Bergman Ramos, London: Sheed and Ward.
Khan, Verity Saifullah, Language Education for all? Chapter 7 of the *Swann Report, Working Paper No.6.* Centre for Multicultural Education, London: Institute of Education.
Steiner, George(1975), *After Babel:* aspects of language and translation. Oxford Press.
Swann, Lord (1985), *Education for all. The report of the Committee of Inquiry into the Education of Children from Minority Ethnic Groups.* London: Her Majesty's Stationery Office.
Tax, Meredith (1972), 'Culture is not neutral, whom does it serve?' In Lee Baxandall (ed.), *Radical Perspectives in the Arts*, Harmondsworth: Penguin, pp. 15-29.
Tylor, E.B. (1871), *Primitive Culture.* London: John Murray.

UNESCO (1976), *Recommendation on participation by the people at large in cultural life and their contribution to it,* adopted by the General Conference at its nineteenth session, Nairobi, 26 Nov. 1976.

UNESCO (1980), *Recommendation concerning the status of the artist,* adopted by the General Conference at its twenty-first session, Belgrade, 27 October 1980.

UNESCO (1982), *Final Report of World Conference on Cultural Policies,* Mexico City, 26 July-6 August 1982.